AFRICANS
in
New Sweden

THE UNTOLD STORY

For the Bowdoin
College. Author's
collection. I'm honored
to add this esteem collection.
HM Muhammad
Class of 1973

AFRICANS
in
New Sweden
THE UNTOLD STORY

By Abdullah R. Muhammad

Wilmington, Delaware

Dedication

I dedicate this book to two very important and instrumental people who are affiliated with the New Sweden Centre of today and whose ancestors were part of the New Sweden Colony of 1640. I make this dedication because it would not have been possible without the leadership and foresight of Herbert Ripley Rambo, past president of the New Sweden Centre and descendent of Peter Gunnarsson Rambo, and Aleasa Hogate, current Vice President and Education Director of the New Sweden Centre and descendent of Anders Larsson Dalbo. Aleasa Hogate's drive, fortitude and tenacity have been vital to the publication of this book. I am eternally grateful to her commitment to this project and the genuine support and concern she has shown throughout.

AFRICANS
in
New Sweden
THE UNTOLD STORY

First Edition

Published by:
Cedar Tree Books, Ltd.
Wilmington, Delaware 19807
books@ctpress.com
www.cedartreebooks.com

ISBN 978-1-892142-56-6
Title: Africans in New Sweden: the Untold Story
Author: Abdullah R. Muhammad
Editor: Nicholas Cerchio
Copy editor: Beverly Cerchio
Cover concept: Aleasa Hogate
Book design: Bob Schwartz

Library of Congress Cataloging-in-Publication Data

Muhammad, Abdullah R.
  Africans in New Sweden: the untold story / by Abdullah R. Muhammad. -- First edition.
    pages cm
  Includes bibliographical references and index.
  ISBN 978-1-892142-56-6
1. African Americans--New Sweden. 2. New Sweden--Race relations. 3. New Sweden--History. 4. Dela-
ware--History--Colonial period, ca. 1600-1775. I. Title.

F167.M83 2013
975.1'00496--dc23

2013006188

Printed and bound in the United States of America

Table of Contents

Foreword

Delaware occupies a unique position on the eastern seaboard of the United States. First settled by Lenape Indians, it became a Swedish colony in 1638. In this year, 2013, we are celebrating the 375th anniversary of that colony. Settlers from Finland, the Netherlands, Germany, France and England added to the mix, as colonial masters came and went. But besides the Europeans, there were also Africans.

Historians have paid little attention to the free and enslaved Africans who shared the land with the Europeans. It may have been because it was unpleasant to see the aristocratic and class society that the Europeans imposed on the American continent, or the fact that so many Europeans had themselves been indentured servants. Whatever the reason, many historians have romantically preferred to see the Europeans as heroic, religious, and freedom-loving rather than as economic exploiters with little evidence of religious core values.

As the historian for the Swedish Colonial Society, its former archivist and governor, I have had an intimate connection with New Sweden history since returning to Pennsylvania in 1996. Also, as the translator and one of the editors of *Colonial Records of Swedish Churches in Pennsylvania*, I have had the privilege of reading both Americana and Swedish scholarship on New Sweden. In my role as advisor to the Board of the New Sweden Centre, I have been intimately involved in Mr. Muhammad's research and the completion of his book.

Since the risk of filiopietism is with all who write about colonial history, which was evident even at both twentieth-century celebrations of the founding of New Sweden, 1938 and 1988, it is refreshing to see Mr. Muhammad's sense of objectivity. The fact that most historians lionized the colonists to avoid any unpleasant sides of their colonial efforts explains why there has been very little objectivity.

Abdullah Muhammad's present book is a needed corrective. What is important about this book is that, for the first time, the history of the Delaware Valley has taken the situation of Africans seriously and documented it. All readers of colonial history and New Sweden history will benefit from this analysis.

Kim-Eric Williams,
Swedish Lecturer, University of Pennsylvania
Historian, Swedish Colonial Society

Introduction

One of the best-kept secrets of the European colonization of the world, particularly of North America, has been the hidden role of Africans—both free and enslaved. The reason for that secrecy was due in large part to the social order and mannerisms of that time period. Commoners (which included servants and slaves) were not written about, unless it was incidental to a report of greater importance. The establishment of the colonies of the east coast of North America—later to be known as the Thirteen Colonies—took root in three major locations, with three major European nations: the English in Virginia, 1607; the English Puritans in Massachusetts, 1620; and the Dutch and Swedes in New York, New Jersey, Pennsylvania, and Delaware, or what was commonly known as the Middle Colonies, from 1626–1638. Not only was this area geographically known as the Middle Colonies, but also it was, literally, sandwiched between two divergent and diametrically opposing English societies—the English Puritans of New England and the English settlers in Virginia sent by the London Company, an enterprise for profit. The former were looking for religious freedom, and the latter were pursuing profit.

Unlike the two English colonies, the Swedes and the Dutch were looking to accomplish both of those objectives, each placing their emphasis differently. The Swedes, however, took full advantage of settling in this new frontier of America and sought to take advantage of all the talents and skills they could find. They befriended the natives of this land and offered freedom through work, rather than a lifetime of forced servitude to their countrymen, to them as well as to Africans and native tribes, in stark contrast to the Dutch, who fought with the native tribes and enslaved and marketed Africans for the sake of profit. It is this unique relationship that existed between the Dutch, Swedes and English as it related to Africans that is the focus of this book. More precisely, it is the social and economic relationship that existed between the Swedes and those who lived in their settlements—commoners, soldiers, farmers, traders, aristocracy, Company men, indentured servants—and free, as well as enslaved Africans, that this research shall attempt to uncover.

For it was within the Swedish colony that the first distinction of a colonist of African origins received any acknowledgement of his presence and his contributions to that community. His name was Antoni Swart, known more commonly as "Black Anthony." The circumstances of his arrival and his life in the Swedish colony gave impetus to this research and the optimistic hope of finding out more about his life and the lives of others like him who existed just below the radar and attentive eye of those charged with recording the people and events of that time.

The most agonizing part of my research has been the acceptance that most of the pertinent records of that time period, particularly those written in Swedish, have been lost to time—the result of battles fought, those in authority choosing to hide certain truths, and ships' logs lost at sea. Nevertheless, records kept by the Dutch and those salvaged by the first conquering English forces under the command of Colonel Richard Nicholls have somehow survived through deliberate acts of preservation and ironic good fortunes of coincidental finds. Furthermore, only a few of our contemporary historians and other authors of historical readings have chosen to sift through the hard-to-read and very boring detailed reports of Colony and Company administrators charged with the task of reporting on life in the colony, to bring overlooked details to light. A few of these historians who did do more digging to find and report on the facts that did not reach the general public and to broaden the view of historic events were Peter Craig, C. A. Weslager, William H. Williams, and John A. Munroe. Without their insightful and scholarly work, much of what I have been able to write would be hollow and very speculative. In fact, one of Delaware's foremost historians, John Munroe, said, "Any work like this history,... is bound to be based in great part on secondary sources—that is, on what has been written previously. Unfortunately, in Delaware historiography, as in the Arabian Desert, there are 'empty quarters,' areas that have hardly been explored. Perhaps this presentation... will stimulate new studies, particularly in areas previously unexamined. Such, at least, is the hope of the author."[1] My sentiments exactly! It was as if he wrote those words specifically for me at this time, not thirty-one years ago as the preface to his book, *History of Delaware*.

Given the enormity of my task, yet the scarcity of recorded facts for that period and for this community of people, I have focused my efforts on the period of 1626–1700, in order to incorporate some important facts relating to the first established Dutch settlement. Much of what I have written about Africans during this period will be the first time a mainstream historical text has revealed such facts and circumstances. With that being said, I have diligently and responsibly noted credible sources to validate my observations and statements of fact. I have taken obvious facts and made logical inferences in order to show a continuum of possible events and circumstances that help explain some missing historical connections.

The commentary that I share in this book is fully sustained by the observations and notations made by others. These comments are necessary in order to show the connection between events that happened and reports that never detailed those events, or reports that did, but were never recovered. I have been careful not to use 21st-century judgment to critique or weigh the merits, good or bad, of the social system that existed during that time period. Just as a person from that period could not possibly understand or accept our social order of today, we cannot be judgmental of theirs. Were there practices during that period that we would find abhorrent? Of course there were. Are they being highlighted in this text for that purpose? Not in the least. What I do highlight is the manner in which the Swedish community, unlike the Dutch and English communities, was able to greatly influence a chain of events that could possibly have set in motion the anti-slavery movement and the end of slavery in this country. To give stature and recognition to a man who looked like all the others being brought and used in this country as chattel labor only, was bold and unprecedented. But, to know that Anthony was not the only one so honored gives significant credibility to the notion that this practice may have been the catalyst for the hard-fought battle to end all forms of slavery in this country and around the world.

As you will see with my opening discussion of the *Swedish View of Slavery*, there was a social mindset among Swedish people that never deviated far from that core belief that men should be free and have a skill to enable them to work to support themselves and their families. Maybe it was that the Swedes were much more literate than average European peasants, who were the bulk of the colonists being sent to settle this new territory. Whatever may be the reason(s), it will be shown that many of the accomplishments of this new world were influenced by Africans who were free men and women, who were never spoken of in mainstream history books. Additionally, I will describe how a consistent social belief by the Swedish people scattered throughout the Middle Colonies helped establish the largest community of free African men and women in the city of Philadelphia, living in the midst of colonial America's largest slave importer—the Dutch—and its greatest slave exploiter—the English.

Those who cannot remember the past
are condemned to repeat it.
George Santayana

1. John Munroe, *History of Delaware*.

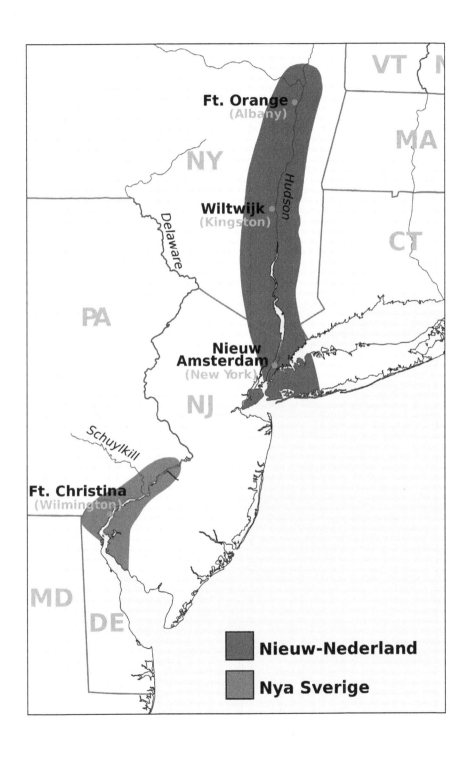

Ft. Orange
(Albany)

VT

MA

NY

Hudson

Wiltwijk
(Kingston)

CT

Delaware

PA

Nieuw
Amsterdam
(New York)

NJ

Schuylkill

Ft. Christina
(Wilmington)

MD

DE

Nieuw-Nederland

Nya Sverige

AFRICANS
in
New Sweden
THE UNTOLD STORY

CHAPTER ONE

Slavery in
the Swedish Community

THE SWEDISH VIEW OF SLAVERY

As we approach the beginning of the 16th century and take a hard look at Swedish society, there is one very salient view that stands in stark contrast to the rest of their European neighbors: Swedes were accustomed to individual freedoms, whereas other Europeans were tied to a class and/or caste system that dominated the poor masses.

Even though the Swedish government was that of a monarchy, the common folks of Sweden were not dominated like their European neighbors. Why is this so important? To understand the Swedish view of slavery, one must understand the acceptable social norms of the society. If a society readily accepted the conditions of forced labor, harsh working conditions, and inequality between people of the same ethnic identity, then it is merely a matter of basic human frailty that these same people would treat people of an ethnic identity inferior to themselves with even greater harshness and stringency. On the other hand, if a nation of people practiced a much different system of labor, personal responsibility, and respect for the basic integrity of all men, then, consequently, their interaction with other ethnic groups would be more in line with what they did normally. In this regard, a Swedish man was proud of being resourceful and hard-working, and actually considered it an insult to have someone do something for him that he could do for himself. Slavery was not a practice of getting everyday tasks completed in Sweden during this time period; instead, it was a form of punishment and retribution for crimes, or for vengeance, or achieving equity for certain social injustices.

Slavery, as a form of forced servitude practiced by the Vikings and other Swedish tribes, was outlawed in 1335 by King Magnus IV,[1] who ruled over Sweden, Norway, and Scandia.[2] Based on the records of that period, slaves or "thralls" as they were known, were the lowest class of Viking society—a class into which people were actually born and which they could not transcend until after they had been freed for at least two generations.[3] This motivation for outlawing slavery was due in large part to the arrival and acceptance of Christianity throughout this region. Traditions and customs that followed this arrival made it "un-Christian-like" to enslave a person who was a Christian or even a "thrall born of Christian parents,"[4] thereby ending the ready supply of slaves.

When we look at the social conditions for social interactions in the rest of Western Europe, we find a pervasive attitude of people using other people who are closest in social standings to their own or below them as a means to enrich or empower themselves. This particular type of slavery brought to this new land, called the Americas, was unique to the "world of slavery." It was not brought as a condition of social ranking, punishment or retribution for a crime, or as a temporary need for added labor, it was the direct result of European expansionism and greed, which other historians simply labeled as "European Colonization." There was literally a "foot race" among Western European nations to see who could colonize the most land in Africa and in the Americas, which included the islands of the West Indies, starting in the early 15th century.[5]

Unlike their European neighbors, Sweden was slow to join the race to colonize and to settle unfamiliar foreign lands.[6] Sweden was not only slow to colonize other territories, but also very late. While other European countries were beginning their exploration for colonization and establishing colonial empires (mid-15th century), Sweden was embroiled in a civil war to determine who would rule all of Sweden, Nor-

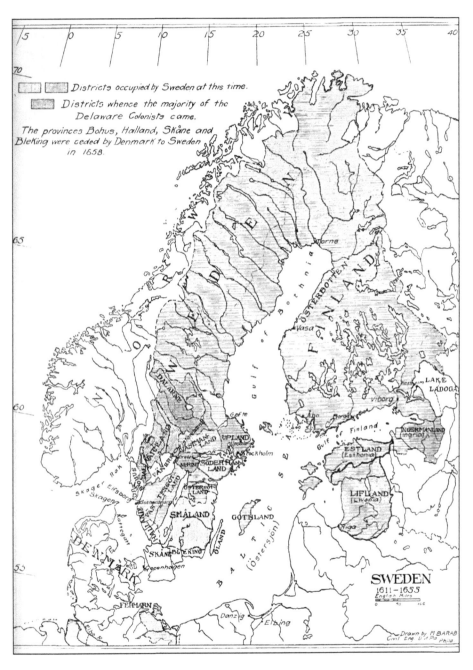

The Swedish Empire at its height in 1658.
(Overseas possessions are not shown).

way, and Denmark.[7] Looking back on the Swedish Empire that proudly recalled its glorious maritime history, few would have imagined that these proud ancient explorers of the seas would be last in exploring for new territories during this time period. Nevertheless, internal feuds among its monarchy and noble classes forced these Scandinavians to focus on building a stronger homefront and maintaining stability.

In addition to being late in its colonization, Sweden's colonization was also very short-lived (1638 – 1663).[8] This, too, helped establish the Swedes' disdainful and non-acceptant view of the harsh enslavement of Africans. By not being among the nations to suffer through decolonization and freedom movements of colonized nations, Sweden as a nation and as a society did not have to endure the hostilities and huge expenses, both in finance and lives, borne by Europe's other colonizers. In fact, beginning in the early 18th century, Sweden took the position of neutrality among the nations, preferring to stay clear of nations at war with their colonists and their hostilities.

In contrast to this enlightened and humanistic view of the treatment of their fellow man, the Swedish Crown, nevertheless, endeavored to establish a profitable presence along the so-called "Gold Coast" of Africa. Why was this undertaken, who were its benefactors, and why and how was it abandoned?

THE RISE AND FALL OF THE SWEDISH AFRICAN COMPANY

Let's begin our examination of this period by answering the question of why this endeavor was undertaken at such a late time—almost 100 years after many European countries, including Sweden's rival, Holland, had already established several colonies. Admittedly, this was a very new and enterprising business venture with some known, but many unknown, risks involved, with prospects for very high profits.

As with many of the other countries looking to cash in on foreign conquests, Sweden's grab for African riches began with the establishment of a private trading company, the Swedish African Company,

The miseries of war depicted in this etching of 1632 entitled: "The Hanging"

founded in 1649.[9] As with all new foreign ventures, an expedition had to be sent to explore and stake out a claim in the new territory. In this case, on April 20, 1650, Henrik Carloff was sent to establish the Company's presence. He successfully purchased a tract of land from the King of Futu along the coast of the Gulf of Guinea, which is now the country of Ghana.[10] This African acquisition was "for the purpose of trade and territorial acquisitions,"[11] to raise much-needed funds to finance Sweden's competition with Denmark in the expanding slave trade to the West Indies and North America. While the Swedish copper mines, which operated from the 10th century until 1992, were financing Sweden's wars of the 16th and 17th centuries, not much of this money, if any, was available for financing imperialistic adventures.

The investors in this enterprise wanted to extract the gold and ivory from Africa to export and trade to their European neighbors; they wanted the rich sugar cane plantations of the Caribbean and the tobacco plantations of the Americas, especially the southern part of North America. They wanted these valuable resources to supply their new colonies, as well as finance more ventures. In addition, they wanted to trade for African slaves from the African interior to send to their Colony (New Sweden), but they lacked both the naval resources

7

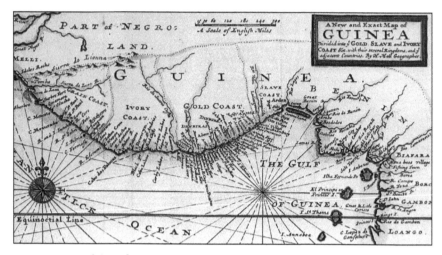

Historic Map of the African Gold Coast

and the tropical experience necessary to get seriously involved in the Atlantic slave trade.[12] The success of this venture was to determine Sweden's far-reaching desire for a "global presence" in other parts of the known world. Even though this ambition had been stalled until now due to the heavy expense of its military battles in the Thirty-Years War,[13] the initial success of this costly undertaking was not enough to sustain the New Sweden Company[14] (which established the first successful permanent settlement in the area, known later as Delaware, in 1638), nor was it enough to retain other African and island acquisitions as a means of furthering its desire to benefit from the African slave trade.

This great ambition for a global presence, the need to compete with the rest of Europe, and its unrealistic involvement in too many areas of interest at the same time caused the unfortunate demise of Sweden's global ambitions. With its physical and financial resources stretched far too thin, these underfunded and poorly supplied companies and their colonies became easy prey to the competing countries of Denmark, the Netherlands, and England. In fact, historical records indicate that the Swedish Gold Coast, under the proprietorship of the Swedish African Company was first sold to the Netherlands by one of Carloff's associates (Schmidt) in March 1659, who reportedly "pocketed the funds" and disappeared. After a successful uprising by the local population against their new unwanted masters and with the help of the King of Futu, the Company directors were able to regain this valuable asset, only to have it taken over by Denmark in 1663.[15]

FORCED LABOR VS. INDENTURED SERVITUDE VS. SLAVERY

Why, you may ask, should I address the matter of distinction between the service of forced labor, indentured servitude, and slavery? Because they are not the same, and the manner in which each community deals with it, in large part, determines how that community will deal with members of other communities. As part of my examination of Africans in New Sweden, this essential question of distinction must be addressed to better understand the "hows" and "whys" of movement of free Africans during this time period.

Captured Africans being herded to slave markets.

The most common difference is generally acepted to be that of time of servitude. Yet, in some cultures, whole social groups are predetermined to have that role of servant or slave, which may or may not be a matter that can be changed by the individual, others in the society, or even the law of the land. As previously stated, "thralls" were considered the lowest class within the Viking social order. They were born into this group and could not transcend to a higher social class, even after being freed from servitude, until at least two generations of the same family had been free.[16] By and large, however, most civilizations considered this difference simply a matter of semantics. After all, there were so many different labels given for the same treatment that it was hard to distinguish one treatment from another. Historically speaking, civilizations throughout time have always had one group based on a salient difference forced to labor or serve the majority of that civilization.

The most significant difference we find between servitude and slavery of any kind historically, compared to this period of European colonization, is the length of service. In Europe, for instance, they saw no difference between serfdom (the life of a lowly peasant farmer), slavery, and servitude; after all, servitude was ubiquitous throughout all of Europe.

The manner of that servitude was that of a dominant group or groups controlling the destiny of a weaker and socially inferior group or groups; whereas during the 17th and 18th centuries, particularly, people neither conquered nor born of an inferior social class were being placed in an artificially created class of servitude.

This new class of servitude was based almost entirely on an ingrained racial and religious prejudice brought by white Christian Europeans to this part of the world. The horror and utter cruelty of this act of enslavement was based on stealing groups of non-servile individuals from their homelands and placing them in a totally foreign environment for the purpose of enriching those who had themselves sprung from meager and/or criminal beginnings.[16a] This brutality sprang originally from a simple need for more cheap labor and led to a grotesque flow of innocent humanity to increase profits and to satisfy an insatiable greed.

What many liberal-minded aristocrats and landowners accepted as a temporary matter of necessity soon became the norm in providing labor needs to highly labor-intensive agricultural productions—such as sugar, tobacco, rice, indigo and, later, cotton.

To better understand how Sweden could be both a bastion for free Africans and other enslaved people, while showing obvious duplicity in the slave trade itself, is to understand the social order and mindset of the people toward labor, service, and enterprise. Make no mistake about it, all of Europe considered slavery and various forms of servitude a necessary and essential element in economic growth and colonization.[17] My discussion here is intended both to clarify certain points as it relates to various forms of service without pay and to ameliorate the readers' limited historical perspective of the need for and use of various forms of servitude, especially as it relates to the founding, operation, and demise of New Sweden. To judge what was done by Sweden during this time period in terms only of the anthropological and sociological concepts of our own time period would be not only unfair to the residents of New Sweden but also a disservice to the purpose of this research.

Even though it may be a necessity for me from time to time to editorialize on the institution of slavery and all of its ills, do not consider that commentary a critique of the people of New Sweden. The intent and goal for that discussion would be to highlight the strength and fortitude of freed Africans to strive against that engrained social mindset in order to live free and to prosper as all other people who were brought to this colony.

Chapter Two

Building New Sweden
Conscience Versus Culture

Necessity, Availability and Acceptability Rule

In the last chapter, I ended by posing a certain conundrum regarding Sweden's role in the Atlantic slave trade that conflicted with its practices at home and in its New Sweden colony. My discussion, for the most part, has not focused on New Sweden (which is the focus of this book) but on the mother country of Sweden. "Why is that?" you ask. The answer, though simple, is marred with certain complexities that stem from the various nationalities of the inhabitants of New Sweden, as well as the set of instructions given to New Sweden's first royal governor, Johan Printz. You see, New Sweden was not founded by Swedes alone, but by a collaboration of Swedes, Dutch, Finns, and a few English. With this in mind, it should be easier to understand

Peter Minuit, 3rd Director-General of New Netherland, and Founder of New Sweden in 1638.

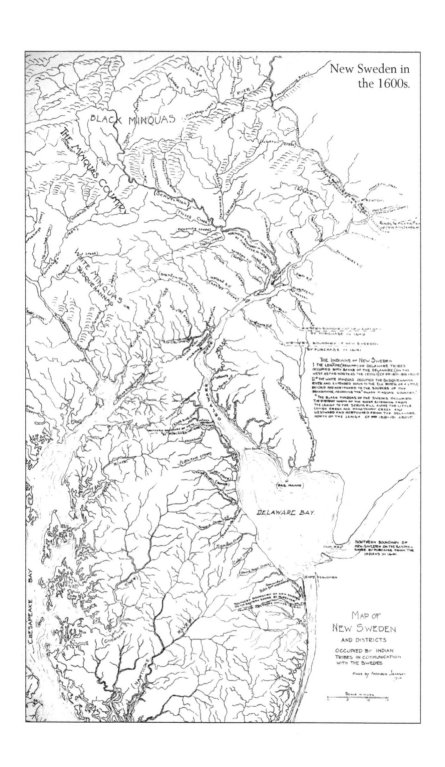

New Sweden in
the 1600s.

Governor Johan Björnsson Printz, first royal governor of New Sweden.

why there were different cultural approaches on how to best establish the settlement of New Sweden. In fact, the colony of New Sweden was first governed by Dutchmen—first, Peter Minuit,[1] the commander of the initial expedition, then, Peter Hollander Ridder, an officer in the Swedish navy, who governed the Colony under Swedish law—which is why I have devoted a good deal of this initial discussion to the workings and dealings of the motherland and the rationale for some decisions by the Colony.

It was not until 1643 that this new colony received an official Swedish governor in the person of Lieutenant Colonel Johan Björnsson Printz, who was sent with an official mandate for seeing to the success of the Colony. By this time, the Swedish government had become much more involved in the business of the Colony because all except one of the principal directors of the New Sweden Company were government officials. So, in effect, the Company was operating more as an arm of the government rather than an independent private enterprise.[2] It was this mandate—a very detailed and specific set of instructions, goals and timelines—that brought about the necessity in New Sweden for more inexpensive labor as quickly as possible.

By reading the directives given to Governor Printz from the Swedish Crown, it is my hope that you will be able to better understand why certain situations developed as they did during Swedish rule along the Delaware:

> *The instructions of Governor Printz, dated Stockholm, August 15, 1642, contain twenty-eight articles, embracing his duties in relation 1st, to the Swedes—2ndly, to the Europeans living in their vicinity—and 3dly, to the Indians. Of these instructions the following is a compendious view. In relation to the Swedes, he was to promote by the most zealous endeavours, a sincere piety, in all respects, towards Almighty God; to maintain the public worship, conformably to the doctrines and rites of the national church [Lutheran Church]; to support a proper ecclesiastical discipline; to urge instruction and virtuous education of the young; to administer justice according to the Swedish laws; to preserve, as far as practicable, the manners and customs of Sweden; to promote diligently all profitable branches of industry—such as the culture of grain—the procuring of good breeds of cattle, in addition to those sent from Sweden—the raising of tobacco as an article of export to the mother country—trafficking with the Indians for peltry [animal furs]—searching for metals and minerals in different parts—looking after valuable kinds of wood— ascertaining what kinds of mulberry trees are best suited for the silk worm—what is the character of the native grapes, and their suitableness for wine—and whether whale and other fisheries may be carried on with advantage, &c. &c. [etc.]. 2ndly, with respect to the Dutch and English in their vicinity; with the first named he was to cultivate a friendly intercourse, but positively to deny their pretended right to any part of the land on the west side of the river, purchased by the Swedes from the Indians, and to prohibit Swedish vessels from passing their fort Nassau: and he was authorised, if all friendly negociation proved fruitless, to repel force by force. Those Dutch families who had settled on the west side, under allegiance to the crown of Sweden, were to retain the granted privileges, but to be advised and persuaded to*

remove further down from the vicinity of Christina Fort, yet not driven away if anxious to remain. The governor was to continue the friendly commercial intercourse with the English in Virginia, then comprehending Maryland, which had already been begun, by supplying their colony with grain, cattle, and other useful articles. Some English families, embracing about sixty persons, having settled, in the preceding year (1641,) on Ferken's creek, (now Salem,) and the agents of the company having, as her majesty's subjects, bought from the Indian owners the whole district from Cape May to Racoon creek, in order to unite these English with the Swedes, the governor was to act faithfully and kindly towards them. And as these English expected soon, by further arrivals to increase their number to several hundred and seemed also willing to be subjects of the Swedish government, he was to receive them under allegiance, though not without endeavouring by gentle means, to effect their removal. 3rdly. Respecting the Indians; the governor was directed to confirm, immediately after his arrival, the treaty with that people, by which they had conveyed to the Swedes the western shore of the Delaware, from Cape Henlopen to the Falls of Sanhickan [or Sankikan] (Trenton,) and as much inland as gradually should be wanted. Also, to ratify the bargain for land on the east side above mentioned; and in these and future purchases, to regard them as the rightful owners of the country. He was to treat all the neighbouring tribes in the most equitable and humane manner, so that no injury, by violence or otherwise, should be done to them by any of his people. He had also in charge to accomplish, as far as practicable, the embracing of Christianity by them, and their adoption of the manners and customs of civilized life.[3]

Governor Printz, as well as other company and government officials, took many approaches to addressing the labor-shortage problem in order to grow the settlement and increase profits. The government began sending more convicted Finns as indentured servants,

Indentured servants tending tobacco plants.

who had been charged with even the least violation of law. In fact, Swedes and Finns alike who could not pay overdue debts were being placed into servitude and sent to New Sweden; however, many were not skilled or equipped to deal with the rigors of being full-time laborers, farmers, or builders.

Faced with this very obvious shortage of unskilled workers, officials turned to forced labor from those in and around the colony, which brings us to the point of availability.

Although Governor Printz was charged with "[treating] all the neighboring tribes in the most equitable and humane manner,"[4] having to force such neighboring tribes as the Minquas, the Lenape, and other native American tribes into servitude to the colony was in no respect humane. In fact, it was not only inhumane, but also not very wise, because Native American men were not capable of completing domestic or agricultural tasks, since those were jobs reserved for the women of the tribe, whom the Swedes did not wish to enslave. Also available for labor were Africans brought in by the Dutch up river and the English from down river in Maryland and Virginia. Unable to buy or trade for the Africans owned by the Dutch or the English, Governor Printz had to use his indentured servants, a few Native Americans, and those Swedes, Finns and Dutchmen who came willingly to make a better life for themselves and their families.

What can arguably be considered as the motivation for establishing the Swedish African Company would be the overwhelming need to send more laborers to New Sweden to accelerate its growth before the Dutch or English, who greatly outnumbered the Swedes, could establish larger colonies to overtake their settlements along the Delaware. It was no secret to the Swedes or the Dutch that the English, who had already established colonies above and below New Netherland and New Sweden along the Delaware, were moving up in a steady flow from colonies in Maryland and Virginia. In addition to the influx of English from the South, there were frequent arrivals of new English settlers from England.

Unlike the Dutch, whose colonization efforts were based almost entirely on profit, or the Swedes, who were having difficulty enticing able-bodied Swedes to come settle this new land, the English were coming in droves, seeking personal and religious freedom. As word began to spread of the wealth and opportunities to be gained in the New World, many more Europeans were finding their way here, but they were coming willingly and, often times, unwillingly to the established colonies of the English. Why? Because the English settlers had made use of African slaves to clear land, plant and harvest many of the New World's money crops, and process them for shipping to England and other parts of the New World. This now brings me to the discussion of acceptability.

During this formable period of settling in North America, no one was debating the moral principles of slavery, nor was anyone defending slavery as a just and morally right practice; instead, the general opinion of using slaves was viewed as a necessary evil that would not last that long.[5] Even by our modern standards, the Swedish approach of dealing with people of other communities would have been considered very liberal in comparison to the manner in which other European countries did so at that time. Nevertheless, the ubiquitous use of slavery and other forms of servitude throughout the known world gave greater motivation to Swedish government officials and entrepreneurs to partake of their share in this growing lucrative labor arrangement. After all, even those only mildly favoring this form of cheap labor justified its use as a temporary means to an end.[6]

Even though many Swedes were eager to take advantage of this growing African trade in human cargo, which was evident by the establishment of the Swedish African Company, there is no written evidence that concludes that the company ever traded or purchased any Africans to be traded as slaves during their entire 13-year possession of the Swedish Gold Coast, but some historians assumed that it happened.[7] From all available documentation, Sweden's limited yet active role in the Atlantic slave trade did not occur again until 121 years later under the leadership of Gustav III in 1784, after he received the island of Saint-Barthélemy as a gift from King Louis XVI. King Gustav III established a Swedish colony on this small eastern Caribbean Island and turned it into a very thriving and prosperous trading center.[8]

A SIGN OF THE TIMES

E ven though there is no conclusive evidence that Sweden ever took an active role in the trading of human cargo for profit, what is very clear is the undeniable acceptance of the role slaves and indentured servants played in developing Europe's westward expansion into the vastness of North and South America and the islands of the Caribbean. Many historical documents give detailed accounts of sugar cane and sugar beet plantations, tobacco plantations, and mills for making molasses and rum. It was the development of these labor-intensive crops and mills which called for a constant flow of manual labor, and it was the greedy, profit-seeking Europeans that called for that free labor.

As I pointed out in the first chapter, servitude of one form or another was being practiced in nearly every part of the known world during this era. In fact, the feudal system of Europe was based upon not only a system of servitude by one group over another, but also a system of social class separation and stratification. With that being said, it should not be hard for any reasonable person to understand how easy it was to sway public opinion of even the most ardent religious Puritans to accepting this harsh and significantly different form of forced servitude. After all, this new form of racial slavery—black Africans from a relatively unknown and non-Christian land—eased the minds of even liberal-thinking Europeans and conservative-minded Christians, like the Swedes, Quakers and Mennonites. In fact, this proverbial phrase eloquently sums up an African view of this convenient European blindness and acquiescence:

No matter how big a stranger's eyes, they cannot see.[9]

The ability of "practicing" and "would-be" slave merchants to justify this life-long form of servitude for non-Christians, who were easily identifiable from white Europeans, greatly accelerated an African slave presence in labor-starved colonial America.

This justification for slavery found a home even among the most liberal and most righteous settlers, which has been confirmed by many historians. One of these historians, Charles Blockson, gave his account of slavery's widespread acceptance during the latter part of the 17th century in this way:

Many prominent Philadelphia merchants and religious and political figures were involved in the trade of African men, women, and children, despite the existence and legal acceptance of the 'peculiar institution' of slavery in the 'City of Brotherly Love'.[10]

21

Swedish settlers, even the religious leaders among them, kept or invited the use of African slaves into their households in the late 17th century when English settlers began arriving and settling in great numbers. In addition to Swedish religious leaders' use of slaves, there were the early Anglican priests and lay members, Quakers, Mennonites and clergymen from the Dutch Reformed Church as well.[11]

Other settlers, who were not able to purchase slaves from the slave markets, took advantage of runaway slaves from Maryland and Virginia plantations. Still others made requests for this hardier labor force from their respective settlement companies—the New Sweden and the Dutch West India Companies. Since animal furs of all types (which required very little labor to acquire) and tobacco (which was very labor-intensive) were the two most profitable commodities of the colonies, it should not be difficult for anyone to understand why these companies were willing to provide slaves. For them, it was all about the "bottom line"—and for the settlers, it was a means to an end. In short, few were here, in these early years, because they wanted a better life for themselves and their families—they came either to get rich or were forced by the rich to come and serve and labor. For Swedish settlers, however, their leadership had been given a set of instructions that precluded them from mistreatment of the indigenous people of this land as well as freedmen from other lands.[12] Nevertheless, the need to accomplish the goals of the government's instructions forced many in the Swedish colony to look beyond the moral issues of their actions and consider the necessity of their actions to achieve their goals. This was the tone of the time that Anthony and others found themselves facing as the Swedish colony and its European neighbors began to grow in numbers.

No Time For Tobacco

As mentioned in the last topic discussion, tobacco was a cash crop to export back to Europe; yet, it was not an easy crop to plant, grow or harvest. In fact, all who came to reap the rewards of this crop made the effort to grow it in large quantities, without fully realizing the amount of labor it took to produce the large quantities needed to meet the demands of the people of Europe. Even though New Sweden maintained three tobacco fields, it could only produce 25-30% of the harvest needed to meet the demands of the Company and the Swedish government. This is why some historians believe that Anthony was brought to this colony to help with the tobacco production. I must whole-heartedly disagree. Given the amount of people (labor) needed in the entire process of planting, cultivating and harvesting tobacco, what could one lone African do? Furthermore, if tobacco production was of such importance to the Company and the government, why was there no mention of this effort in the reports and letters sent by Governor Printz or his predecessor? Surely, if Anthony was vital to the increased production of this cash crop, why are there no progress reports of this effort mentioned by historians?

There is absolutely no disputing the omnipotent importance of tobacco during the colonizing period of North America. It rapidly became the most staple of staple crops the world had ever known.[13] Its value as a cash crop was virtually unequaled during this period— a value made even greater by the almost unending demand for it throughout Europe. If I were to compare it to a cash crop of to-day (even though there is no true comparison), I would have to say marijuana, if it was legalized. But like marijuana, many people did not condone or promote its popularity among the masses. One case in point was the ability of Sir Francis Drake and Sir Walter Raleigh to popularize tobacco (also nicknamed the "jovial weed" by Francis Drake) among the English upper class in the late 16th century. Yet, in total opposition to that popularity, King James was one of the harshest critics of smoking tobacco:

Sounding like a modern [day] physician, James anonymously published 'Counterblast to Tobacco' in which he described smoking as a custom loathsome to the eye, hateful to the nose, harmful to the brain, dangerous to the lungs, and in the black stinking fumes thereof, nearest resembling the horrible stygian smoke of the pit that is bottomless.[14]

In spite of his dire warning as the head of the government, English society imported more and more of this "habit-forming" plant.

Another case in point, the Swedish government stated in 1639 that "if they had been a more careful government they would have banned the use of tobacco altogether among its people due to its negative effects on the people in general." Since the wording of that ordinance reads like something from our legislators of today, I have printed it in its entirety below:

> *We Christina etc. make hereby known, Whereas We see and understand, that this Our State and Kingdom is by one and the other, without order and judgment, being flooded with tobacco, a merchandise, which until some time ago has been unknown here and besides in itself is not very useful, but nevertheless is now bought and consumed by the common people to such an extent, that it has become an abuse and in a great measure brings great injury and poverty on many, and although it would not be unjust, if We as a careful Government were to forbid altogether the importation into Our Kingdom of the said tobacco and thereby in time prevent, that the means of Our faithful subjects further go out of the Kingdom for such an unnecessary commodity to their final considerable injury and loss of property, yet, because this general bad habit and great abuse are practiced by almost everybody and because at present We consider it injudicious to prohibit and abolish it entirely; Therefore We have been moved, to restrict it somewhat and adapt it to the circumstances of the times and the humor of the people...*[15]

Nevertheless, the Swedish government, like all the other colonizing countries of Europe, wanted to realize a profit from its investment in this new enterprise of settling the land of North America. The popularity and profitability of the tobacco crop almost necessitated the need to grow as much of it as possible. When Johan Printz was installed as New Sweden's first royal governor and armed with a set of instructions for governing and making the colony profitable, which were at times at odds with reality in the colony, he quickly established three large tobacco plantations and several smaller ones, which in no way rivaled the production or quality of tobacco grown in Virginia. In order to establish these farms quickly during the growing season, Printz ordered Swedish and Finnish farmers to convert their "corn fields" into "tobacco plantations," even though few, if any, had any knowledgeable experience in dealing with this new crop. As for the loss of the corn to use as food, he arranged to buy the corn from the Lenape, "who cultivated extensive [corn] fields near their villages." The largest of these plantations was in Upland, under the direction of an expert planter (possibly an Englishman) and a labor crew of twelve men. The second largest plantation was in the vicinity of Fort Christina with eleven planters working the fields, and the third was on the Schuylkill River, most probably New Korsholm (Cross Island) with only seven workers. Yet, even with all those men and resources dedicated to the growing of this cash crop, New Sweden still had to buy the bulk of its tobacco from Virginia farmers to meet its shipment to Sweden.[16]

Essentially, "there were two major kinds of tobacco present in the Chesapeake colonies (along the Chesapeake and Delaware Bays); Oronoco and Sweetscented."[17] The tobacco that was grown the most in the colonies—including New Sweden—(Oronoco) was not the most preferred in Europe. The preferred tobacco, Sweetscented, was grown almost exclusively in Virginia along the banks of the James, York, Rappahannock, and Potomac Rivers, and it had a milder taste and greater market value. With this being the case, it's easier to understand why most of the tobacco sent to Sweden came from Virginia and not from New Sweden. Furthermore, during the period of Swedish rule in the Delaware River Valley, there was not nearly enough labor available to keep up with, let alone increase, the production of tobacco at these farms. As pointed out in the following excerpt, tobacco was very labor-intensive and lacked any utilitarian value outside of its "cash crop" value. Well-known Delaware historian, C. A. Weslager, gave this quoted explanation from his book on the Swedish colony:

> Although less strenuous than many other occupations, tobacco production was not without its anxieties and dangers. The planter always ran the risk of crop failure, loss from improper curing and prizing. This detailed attention caused a laborer to cultivate no more than 3 or 4 acres of plants. In addition, like other agricultural products, tobacco was greatly affected by the weather. A dry spell in the spring or fall delayed planting. On the other hand, an extreme wet spell drowned the tobacco and ruined the crop by causing the leaves to spot.
>
> It neither supplied food to him nor fodder to his beasts; it could not yield him roof-timber nor firewood. He had to shelter, watch over, nurse it at every stage of growth and curing, for never was there a more tender plant or one subject to a greater variety of plagues, diseases, and disasters. The preparation and sowing of a tobacco seed bed was a process as elaborate as the making of pillow-lace; the weather, a fly, a dozen various accidents, may have defeated a planter's prospects of a supply of plants. Not until the summer came, after a year of growing the delicate tobacco and until seventeen months had elapsed, were the planter's troubles over. Then at last he brought his crop to market, had it sampled, and sold it for half the price he expected to get for it.[18]

Instead, Governor Printz, and then later Johan Risingh (who led the colony after Printz' departure to Sweden) found themselves fending off Dutch aggression and intrusion, rather than spending time cultivating profitability in the colony for the New Sweden

Company and Swedish Government. With these facts in mind, it should be easier for you to see why I've concluded that there was "no time for tobacco."

CHAPTER THREE

The Role of Africans in New Sweden

THE FIRST LONE AFRICAN – ANTHONY

On March 29, 1638, the first wave of settlers from Sweden, commanded by Peter Minuit, a German-born Dutch resident and former director of the Dutch New Netherland, came ashore on the banks of the Christina River (often referred to as "the Rocks") to start what was to become the first permanent settlement of Europeans along the Delaware River.

Although a previous attempt to start a permanent settlement was made by the Dutch as early as 1631 in the area known today as Lewes, that effort suffered a great disaster—all 32 Dutch colonists (all men) were killed by the Sickoneysinck, a branch of the Lenape tribe of Native Americans in that area.

Even though there is a story to explain what happened to these ill-fated men, the reality of the story's claim is and has been very dubious to many historians, myself included. One of those prominent historians, Thomas J. Scharf, explained it this way in his book, *History of Delaware, 1609-1888*:

> *Just how the massacre of the settlers came about was never known, but there is reason to believe that it was incited by wrongful or at least unwise acts on the part of Hossett and his men.*[1]

Map of Spanish Caribbean.

As for the first shipload of settlers to New Sweden (most of whom were Dutch and Finns), none of the 25 soldiers left behind with Mans Kling (a Swedish officer left in charge by Peter Minuit) made their landing or their stay permanent. In fact, it was not until the return of *Vogel Grip* (January, 1639) from its unsuccessful trade for tobacco in Jamestown, Virginia, and its attempt at plundering a Spanish ship for its gold and/or silver in the thriving shipping channels of the Spanish Caribbean, that the very young settlement of New Sweden actually acquired its second permanent resident and its first African settler,[2] Anthony Swart, better known as "Black Anthony." For it was this lone African, who was acquired by unknown methods and for a sum just as unknown and for reasons furthermore unknown, who became the first of all those like him, who survived the journey across the ocean, to make this new-found area a place to call his home.

In my opinion, much is unknown about the exact where, why, how, and how much it took to secure Anthony, because it is clear from the reports and letters to Swedish officials that this was an unauthorized trip by its skipper, Captain Andreas Juransson (also written as Andrian Joransen), who apparently kept most of the details of this journey from being revealed to those at the New Sweden Company as indicated in the following excerpt from a report archived at the Royal Archive at Stockholm:

> *We know little about this expedition of the Grip years afterwards, the skipper was accused of [sailing about the West Indian waters looking for Spanish treasure] doing it all for his own benefit, and the only addition it brought to the colony's wealth, that we discovered, was a negro slave.*[3]
>
> NEW SWEDEN HISTORY,
> ROYAL ARCHIVE AT STOCKHOLM, VOL. II, CHAPT. LXIII

Nevertheless, there is enough circumstantial evidence to suggest that Anthony was perhaps taken from a Spanish ship in the West Indies (better known during that period as the Spanish Caribbean) because of his seafaring skills. It is a well-known fact that many Africans along the west coast of Africa (his suspected home) and those who had spent a reasonable amount of time on islands in the West Indies and the East Atlantic Islands had either acquired their special seafaring skills from the elders in their village or after being forced to man such positions as cabin boys, boatmen, cooks, rowers, etc., as a result of their captivity.[4] Perhaps the captain was considering the timely value of having a skilled seaman like Anthony in New Sweden. After all, a man of those skills was needed to navigate the waters of the Delaware River Valley, with its network of rivers and streams. Furthermore, Africans were common at sea in almost every seafaring position and were employed on European ships well before the discovery of North America.[5]

What is known, and known for certain, is that Anthony was the only member of the passengers and crew of *Vogel Grip (Bird Grif-*

fin) and of *Kalmar Nyckel's* first journey to the Delaware River Valley (originally called South River by the Dutch) who stayed almost until the very end of Swedish government rule. The importance of that fact establishes the long-term significance of Anthony's presence among the Swedes and other settlers of New Sweden.

By all accounts, Antoni Swart (aka Black Anthony) possibly greeted every colonist to this settlement, by being something of a 'fixture' in this small, close-knit and struggling community. The fact is, Anthony was already fully established in New Sweden after living there nearly 15 months before the second landing of *Kalmar Nyckel (Key of Kalmar)* in April, 1640. Yet, even with all of his advance presence and his painfully obvious complexion and cultural difference, there are no indications that he is ever mentioned in reports or letters sent back to Sweden or to any Company officials. And what is even more unsettling about this lack of attention to Anthony is the fact that Lindström in just a casual stopover in the Canary Islands saw fit to mention a Negro slave attendant,[6] but does not mention the presence or absence of New Sweden's most famous African, after his arrival in New Sweden. I will come back to that thought in due time.

As for this second landing of *Kalmar Nyckel*, under the leadership of Peter Hollander Ridder (governor of New Sweden from 1640 to 1643, which included women and children), Swedes resolutely began the process of establishing a permanent settlement. Further actions taken by the Swedish government to buy back Dutch shares in the New Sweden Company and to satisfy all Dutch claims to payments due were made possible by using funds available from the Old South Company—established some 15 years earlier when this commercial enterprise was first discussed—which fully established Sweden's decision to take ownership of this venture and to make it a successful and self-reliant Swedish colony in North America.[7] By 1641, Dutch stockholders had sold out all of their interest, making the New Sweden Company a fully-owned Swedish enterprise; and by the start of 1642, the Company was practically operating as an arm of the Swedish government.[8] This is an important fact at this point in our discussion, because it should have established that the treatment of Africans from this point on should mirror the social conscientiousness of the Swedish government and its citizens. Also, it is worth noting that none of the reference sources I have used for this research include any discussions or any reference to Black Anthony during this period of Governor Ridder's leadership.

Since Anthony was a member of the founding crew of men left with the task of carving out a village stronghold that would support a Swedish colony, it would seem reasonable to assume that his contributions should have been singled out by virtue of his lone standing; yet, there are no indications of that, as I have already mentioned. Even though Anthony watched and inevitably helped many new arrivals get settled into their new surroundings and to adjust to life along the Delaware for four years prior to the installation of Johan Printz (New Sweden's first royal governor), it was as if he did not exist as a valued member of that community. Again I ask the question, "how can someone so obviously different from everyone else in the colony not get mentioned in reports or letters, if not just incidentally?" In light of all that was happening to populate New Sweden and to furnish her with skilled workers and farmers (which I will discuss in much more detail in the next chapter), it was Anthony who somehow proved himself capable and valuable enough to be selected as a special assistant, sloop pilot, and resident of the first royal governor's estate; yet, again, there is no mention of this "trusted African sloop pilot" or the Governor's "Negro servant who was always at his side," or the "lone African known as Black Anthony."

One historian, Dr. William H. Williams, stated that Anthony, while living on Tinicum Island at Governor Printz' estate, "cut hay for the governor's cattle and worked on Printz' little sloop." Dr. Williams further states that Company records indicate that Anthony was still a member of New Sweden as late as 1654, by evidence of several purchases he made during that year from the commercial company that ran the settlement. He even indicates in his book that Anthony was probably a free man at that time by virtue of his ability to buy goods for himself.[9] Yet how does this happen when there is no mention of him in Swedish correspondence from 1639 to 1643? How and why does this man go from virtual obscurity to holding an important position in the colony? Even though several historians agree that Anthony was either granted his freedom just prior to Johan Printz' arrival or just after his arrival, there is no mention of him among the freedmen in the colony. How do we know this? We know that his name did not appear on any lists of freedmen in the colony under Governor Printz' leadership or during Johan Rising's command, and there were several occasions for him to sign or make his mark.[10]

Again, due to the lack of adequate first-hand accounts or reports to the contrary, we are left to speculate as to why Black Anthony's name does not appear alongside other freedmen in the colony. In considering what is and what is not possible based on known facts, I am inclined to accept the belief of my fellow historians that Anthony was a free man at a given point during Swedish rule of the colony. Yet there do not appear to be any surviving records or papers that document a date-certain for his release from servitude, which was an indentured servitude placed on him in order to repay the cost of gaining his freedom from his captors in the Spanish Caribbean. Furthermore, Swedish law also documented the fact that Anthony must have been free by that time, because he could only be held in servitude for a maximum of six years. Here is an excerpt from the outline of the law from well-known Swedish historian Amandus Johnson in his book on Swedish settlements:

> 8. *Whoever hires from the company an indentured servant over fourteen years of age shall give, besides the said transportation money, additional twenty-four riksdaler and then the servant shall serve him in six consecutive years. The servant shall annually be given board, shoes and shirts. After six years of service an indentured servant shall be entirely free, etc.*
>
> 9. *If an indentured servant has served the company here in the country a year more or less, then so much of the servant's time and*

*service shall be deducted from his second engagement in order that
an indentured servant may become free after six years, etc.*[11]

On the other hand, it is reasonable to suggest that his name did
not appear on any of the lists for freedmen or residents if a freeman
had to own land and a resident had to be married to a land-owning
freeman. The fact that Anthony lived at Printzhof (Governor Printz'
estate on the island of Tinicum) and was free to move about the
Colony could also suggest that he was a tenant at that location either
with a financial obligation to pay his own way or to work for his land,
food, and shelter in lieu of payments. In either situation, if he were
a tenant, and he was not given his own land and certain other privi-
leges when Governor Printz left New Sweden in the Fall of 1653, it
is reasonable to assume that the last record of Anthony's presence
in New Sweden at the Company store gathering supplies was his
preparation to leave the colony.

At any rate, if the records confirm Anthony's presence in the Colony in 1654, then we can safely conclude that he was not a part of Governor Printz' party of 25 settlers and soldiers who went with him to
New Amsterdam to take a Dutch ship back to Europe.[12] At the same
time, it is not at all clear whether he left as a part of the group of 15
men (some with their families) who deserted to the English colonies
in Maryland;[13] however, if this group left by boat, there is a high prob-
ability that Anthony may have been the skipper of their vessel. Additionally, if he was aware of other free Africans who were living in the
coastal areas of Maryland and Virginia, who (like himself) had completed their service as indentured servants or had been manumitted
and were now living as free men,[14] then he had an incentive to make
the trip. Unlike the colonies along the Delaware River, the Maryland
and Virginia colonies had much larger populations and a much larger
population of Africans (the vast majority of whom were slaves).

Another possibility to consider (if Anthony did in fact leave with
this group of deserters) is the likelihood that he may have been one
of the two beheaded by the Indians hired by Johan Papegoja "to bring

them back" to Fort Christina. There is no record of the names of the settlers who were killed, but Dr. Peter Craig's investigation of this event has assumed that it most likely included Matts Hanson, who was one of the leaders of that expedition. Even though there was a partial list of those who deserted without Papegoja's permission—some being Company men with debts owing and some others being soldiers, who would've faced dire consequences for deserting—it's unlikely that Anthony was among them.[15]

Was there a reason Anthony's name and presence were conveniently excluded from reports to Sweden and other company officials? Could he have been someone of importance who was kidnapped by the captain of *Vogel Grip*? The obvious veil of the unknown that covers almost all of the circumstances regarding Anthony's apprehension and his journey to New Sweden leaves many more questions than answers.

THE NEED FOR SKILLED LABOR

There is every reason to believe, based on the historical accounts I have read, that Antoni Swart (Black Anthony) was brought to this emerging colony of New Sweden based on his skills. There is an abundance of circumstantial evidence, but no conclusive documentation has been found that confirms this conclusion; yet all of the documentation which is known strongly suggests this as a valid inference. Why? Well, consider what is known: first, we know that Captain Juransson, captain of *Vogel Grip* which first traveled to Virginia then to the West Indies, had not had any success with those two trading missions. As captain on a mission, he could not afford to go back to the colony, then to Sweden empty-handed; therefore, he did what he had to do to make sure that did not happen. Just what he had to do and exactly what and how he did it was not a part of any surviving records. Whatever Peter Minuit may have written in his journal about this matter was regrettably lost at sea along with him, when he sailed to the island of St. Christopher and was lost in a violent storm aboard the ship of another captain. Whatever the captain of the *Vogel Grip* wrote, it is very questionable that it was all of the truth, and we know that it was not promptly submitted to his superiors, based on the following passage from a report by officials of the New Sweden Company:

> *We know little about this expedition of the 'Grip' [until] years afterwards...*[16]

Secondly, we know that the captain is keenly aware of the fact that the small contingency left on the Minquas Kill (the Christina River as it was known by the Dutch) was left with the task of establishing the foundations of a permanent settlement. This task, of course, required men of skill in many different areas. If the captain was going to make a trade for something, it had to be someone of great value or of a great usefulness. Finally, we know that after Anthony arrived at New Sweden, he was one of two to stay and help others to build, establish the colony and to be given the position of serving at the side of the first royal governor of the colony.

A little over a year after Anthony and the crew had nestled in at Fort Christina, the second expedition of *Kalmar Nyckel*, under the command of Peter Hollander Ridder (also a Dutchman), arrived at the fort on April 17, 1640, with some artisans and their wives and children, but not nearly enough. Just as the first landing of *Kalmar Nyckel* brought mainly sailors and soldiers who were not skilled or capable of building a sustainable community, Ridder felt that his shipload of colonists were just as incapable of laying a strong building foundation. Ridder complained that he "did not find his colonists very handy, for he...had no one capable of building a common peasant's house."[17] Even though preparations had been made to send over needed craftsmen and artisans to help build a strong village structure for the colony, the following excerpt from Amandus Johnson tells otherwise:

> *Governor Hindrickson of Elfsborg was especially requested to engage some artisans, such as blacksmiths, shoemakers, brick-*

makers, carpenters and others, three or four of them to be married, who should take their wives along to cook, make beer and wash for the settlers. As it was difficult to find people willing to migrate on their own accord, it was decided to deport to America, with their families and property, deserted soldiers and others, who had committed some slight misdemeanor. After one or two years they were allowed to return, if they so desired.[18]

As stated in the excerpt above, plans were made to supply the new colony with the necessary personnel to build a strong structural foundation, but too few were willing to make the journey or to leave their homes. Consequently, those who were willing, along with those who were sent against their wishes, numbered more as farmers and general laborers than as skilled craftsmen and artisans. What is also true is the reluctance of the Dutch stockholders to fund adequately this second expedition, since the first expedition was such a "losing proposition." The fact that sailors had to be paid two months' wages in advance, instead of waiting to be paid upon their return, was another indication of the distrust in the viability of this expedition.[19]

SOCIAL STATUS VERSUS WORK STATUS

So far, I have examined New Sweden's first African in the colony, Anthony, and I will discuss in more detail the presence of other Africans who were brought to the colony as skilled labor in the following chapters. It is very clear and unequivocal that other Africans were brought to the colony to provide skilled labor in areas underserved by the settlers who were brought there. These Africans that I speak of were supplied by the Dutch of New Amsterdam to Dutch farmers living within the Delaware River Valley. Most of the settlers who came prior to Johan Rising were soldiers, sailors, farmers, and woodsmen. A few craftsmen came in April 1640 with Ridder, but their numbers were far too few to build the homes and other buildings needed to house and maintain that growing community. As a result, landowners from Maryland and Virginia began to settle along the southern Delaware River coastal areas, taking advantage of the unsettled rich farm areas where land was plentiful and virgin and still very rich in nutrients. After 1648, these same landowners brought their African servants and slaves to this area which helped introduce large groups of Africans to the people of New Sweden.

Some of these small farmers and moderate landowners made their way as far north as New Sweden, along with their small but talented group of African slaves and servants. At other times, only the slaves or freed servants made their way to the Swedish colony, bringing with them their God-given skills and those acquired during their captivity. Many of these skills, which far exceeded the abilities of the average European (who mastered only one or two skills), were mastered by African servants only by way of observation. They would be able to watch as these skills were performed by European craftsmen, and then quickly imitate those same skills. At other times, based on the needs of their masters, they would be forced to learn certain skills in order to increase their value and worthiness. At any rate, many of those "multi-talented" Africans were some of the first to test their skills out on their own, and they became some of the first runaways. Here is an example of how some of those Africans were described:

> *A runaway named Deadfoot was described as an indifferent shoemaker, a good butcher, ploughman, and carter; an excellent sawyer, and waterman, and understands breaking oxen well, and is one of the best scythemen…; so ingenious a Fellow, that he can turn his hand to anything.*[20]

Yet, no matter how many skills or talents most black African servants possessed, they were never equal to other servants or freedmen. In isolated incidents talented African servants were able to win their freedom, along with substantial amounts of land and property, because of the wealth and prestige their skills and talents brought to their owners. But, as the quote above indicates and what much of history has shown, many bonded Africans, convinced that they could make it on their own with their many skills, became runaways.

We know all too well of the talents that Anthony Swart (Black Anthony) brought to New Sweden and its first royal governor; yet, for all of American history, it is as if he never existed. In fact, most Swedish historians neglected his presence and his existence during that period. If not for the work of one or two historians, many of us (including this writer) would not have heard of Anthony. Yes, it is true that servants and the common people did not get mentioned in the reporting letters and journals of that era, but his uniqueness and his position in the colony should have warranted much more acknowledgement. The failure to include Anthony (if no more than a side-note) when relating the story of Governor Printz is not a clear matter of social indifference to that era, as much as it could be of social prejudice of the writers' era relating the history. Without question, the social order of that society was much different from ours in how it related to members of its community…or was it? Do we not undermine and overlook the worthiness of common people while loudly proclaiming the virtues and trivial activities of the wealthy and celebrated members of today's societies?

The Swedish colonies, as well as the Dutch and English colonies, were all started by companies looking to enrich themselves through the brave and arduous efforts of many common folks and servants. It was clear then as it still is today that the worth of a man is measured by his productivity and usefulness to the company, not by his worth as a human being. By and large, your work status greatly supersedes your social status. This leads me to conclude that it was not the type of society that established the status of working people, but the type of social order that was in place within that society. In short, during the building of New Sweden, it was not the society that determined who was mentioned in the journals and records of that time, but the Company and government officials who were responsible for the success of that society.

CHAPTER FOUR

What Became of Antoni Swart and Others Like Him?

THE DILEMMA OF BEING AFRICAN

I n the early stages of establishing New Sweden and other colonies along the Delaware River, there was very little need for large quantities of cheap labor because the financial interests of the New Sweden Company, the Dutch West India Company and the English settlers to the north depended on the fur trade and modest agriculture. Among the agricultural crops being grown in the New World, one in particular, tobacco, was becoming very popular back in Europe and the demand for it was producing great profits. As the tobacco trade began to increase exponentially, so did the profits. Suddenly, this very profitable crop caused all of the European colonies to rush to find ways to grow and harvest it successfully, even though it was extremely limited in its overall social and agricultural utility. Outside of being a cash crop based on the public's demand for it, it had no other residual social benefit.

Nevertheless, one area in particular—Virginia—exploded with increased tobacco harvesting. Not only did this area harvest more tobacco than anywhere else in the New World, but it also produced the most preferred tobacco—Sweetscented. Production outputs of this crop went from a very modest 60,000 pounds in 1622 to over 1.5 million pounds by the time Black Anthony arrived in New Sweden.[1] Incidentally, many historians accept the well-circulated but unconfirmed theory that Anthony was brought to the Swedish colony for the sole purpose of helping to grow tobacco. If it was clearly understood by all those who have accepted that theory as fact, it was obviously not understood by them how extremely labor-intensive that crop production was from start to finish. It is that fact and that fact alone that initiated the start of one of the most inhumane practices of transport and treatment of human beings the modern world has ever known.

What started in 1619 with only 20 Africans brought to Virginia, who were treated more as indentured servants than slaves,[2] ended only after the conclusion of America's bloodiest war—the Civil War. And during the time period between 1619 and 1700, all of the colonies along the Delaware were affected by the increasing number of Africans who were brought to Maryland, Virginia and Philadelphia to provide the cheap and plentiful labor force that the colonial agrarian, retail and unmechanized industrial communities needed.[3] That influx of black Africans to these shores created a subculture that stereotyped every African ever brought here, particularly those who were freedmen, either by birth or manumission. After 1700, which is not the period of focus for this book, slavery along the Delaware grew exponentially in all of the English-ruled colonies.

This brings us to the conundrum of Anthony's existence in New Sweden, which began with the mysterious circumstances that brought him to the colony and ended with his equally mysterious disappearance from the colony. During his stay in New Sweden he was everywhere, yet he was nowhere. In other words, little has been written of him assisting Governor Printz at the governor's estate, Printzhof. Furthermore, hardly any written records, letters or reports openly acknowledged his presence. Likewise, from court records and reports we know that there were other Africans in New Sweden, because Dutch settlers living there used company-owned slaves as servants and farm workers[4] whom they acquired from the Dutch West India Company. Very little is known and even less has been included in the history books of Dutch and Swedish historians revealing the existence and practice of slavery in New Netherland and New Sweden; but it is documented that the first supply of African slaves—eleven men pirated from Spanish and Portuguese ships—was brought to New Amsterdam as early as 1625.[5] In fact, three years before Anthony had been brought to the South River, Dutch privateers[6] along with slave ships from Dutch Caribbean islands brought roughly 2,300 Africans to this area. In addition, William D. Piersen in his book *From Africa to America* maintains that the early Swedish colonists along the Delaware Bay were persuaded by the Dutch use of African bondsmen in their labor force and soon followed the Dutch lead by adding Africans and Native Americans to the Company's labor crews.[7] Hollanders who were convicted of criminal offenses in New Netherland were routinely sent to the South River (Delaware River area) to serve out their sentences as laborers with the company blacks (African slaves) as indicated in the following excerpt from the Albany Records:

> *On February 3, 1639, a judgment is obtained, before the authorities at Manhattan, against one Coinclisse, for wounding a soldier at Fort Amsterdam. He is condemned to serve the company, along with the blacks, to be sent by the first ship to South River, pay a fine to the fiscal, and damages to the wounded soldier.[8]*

By all historical accounts, this appears to be the first documented confirmation that Africans were in the area of New Sweden forts and settlements. The Company slaves (who were brought to the colony in greater numbers starting in 1646)[9] were brought to New Netherland (New Amsterdam) from Dutch colonies in the Caribbean and South America (Curacao and Brazil) as well as by Dutch slave traders to North America. And long before Sweden began a practice of sending its criminals to North America in 1653, the Dutch had been doing it for years in an effort to populate their colonies and forts. So, for the most part, settlements along the Delaware became a place of banishment for both Dutch, then later, Swedish and Finnish criminals who were condemned to work as indentured servants with Africans doing menial labor. The following excerpt from the pages of *Blacks in Colonial America* indicates some of the work that the company slaves performed:

> *These men cut timber, burned lime, and built Fort Amsterdam at the southern tip of Manhattan, while others worked in agriculture. Some blacks may have fought alongside their white masters against the Indians, but they were probably baggage handlers and support troops rather than actual combatants. The slaves were under the supervision of an employee of the company, the 'Overseer of Negroes,' who received 25 florins each month and 100 florins in 'board money.' Two years after the introduction of male slaves, three black females were introduced into the colony.*
>
> *They were used as household help by the executives of the company.[10]*

The following passage from the Royal Swedish Archive in Stockholm details the case of one of the first convicted felons in Sweden who was sentenced for attacking and wounding a soldier and sent to New Sweden, an action which was personally approved by the Queen in 1653:

> *The Fiscal's demand on and against Gysbert C. Beyer in having been seen and everything being maturely considered, he is condemned to work with the Colony's Blacks, until the 1st sloop shall sail for the Southriver, where he is to serve the Company and pay the wounded soldier fl 15, the surgeon fl 10 for his fee and the Fiscal a fine of fl 10.[11]*

Although there is no mention of African slaves in New Sweden, it is conclusive from the excerpt above that there existed more than one slave and that they belonged and worked for the betterment of the colony, just as they did in New Netherland. Bearing these facts in mind, it should be easier to see why any freed African, especially Anthony, would have a harder time moving freely outside the confines of New Sweden, where he was widely known and accepted.[12]

Throughout my research a consistent pattern emerged regarding the presence of Africans—they were only mentioned in matters of possessions and in matters of punishment. Even though Anthony occupied a very noticeable presence at the side of a prominent individual, Governor Printz, he still was not given an individual identity. For the most part, Africans who came to all of the colonies in this area, particularly in Maryland and Virginia, came in response to a labor shortage. As the colonies along the Delaware grew (aided by generous land grants from the British government), the need for more labor grew as well. Thus began a growing population of African slaves and servants that soon became a population of free Africans. Nevertheless, free or enslaved, very little public attention was given to this basically servile group, just as little attention was given to the white indentured servant. However, there was a significant basic difference—the ability of one to blend in, while the other stood out. Africans stood out not only physically but also culturally—in how they lived and worshiped. It is the recognition of this salient difference that created the dilemma for each and every African living among Europeans—the Dutch, English and Swedes. In the matters of state, Africans simply were not considered above issues of property or violations of law.

The real dilemma for Anthony and other Africans in these servant-dependent colonies was the distinction that was made between black and white runaway servants. As early as 1640 in Virginia, some African servants had already become bond servants for life, whereas others were given this "life-long" servitude as punishment for running away. In contrast, European runaway servants were sentenced "to serve their master [only] one additional year."[13] To add to African servants' dilemma was the first law that recognized slavery as a legitimate enterprise, which was passed by Massachusetts in 1641.[14]

The enactment of that law set a precedent for the treatment of black servants in every colony. No longer could Anthony or any other African, free or in servitude, move about as freely or with any confidence that their rights would be respected and protected. Now that slavery and Africans were considered one-in-the-same (by society, not the courts), even free Africans who moved about on their own would no longer be safe from those chasing runaway slaves and servants. Why? Because free Africans who did not have any documents to prove that they had been freed or that they were free, could be captured by unscrupulous "bounty hunters" or "slave chasers" and sold into slavery. Without the protective oversight or companionship of European freedmen or indentured servants, Africans who could not speak the dominant language—Swedish, Dutch, English or Spanish—would have been hard-pressed to find a safe haven during Anthony's time. After all, indentured servitude and slavery were practiced in all parts of the existing colonies—north and south.[15]

Could this widening net of an increasing population of entrenched African servants and slaves have caused Anthony to "drop out of sight" in 1654? In the absence of Governor Printz, who did not take Anthony with him back to Sweden nor give anyone an indication of what was going to happen to the Colony, Anthony probably did not know what was going to become of himself. Whatever land and personal property he possessed, he could not have felt comfortable with maintaining it in the same way he had under the governor, knowing that the governor's daughter and son-in-law were going to take control of Tenecum (Tinicum)—the island estate. After all, the governor's daughter, Armgard Papegoja, was known for being a stern task-master. Also knowing that the Dutch, who were responsible for nearly all, if not all, of the African slaves who were in and around the Colony,[16] were about to capture and/or dominate the area, Anthony must have felt a pressing need to leave his present situation.

The most unfortunate reality at this point in trying to determine what became of Anthony is really anybody's guess. There are no hinted leads, no "smoking-gun" trails, nor any hidden clues—Anthony is a classic case of here today and gone tomorrow. Based on what is known, all of the following are realistic possibilities as to what became of Anthony:

1. My most promising and wishful expectation is that he left the Colony because he no longer felt safe from being enslaved or being forced back into some degree of servitude. He may have left with the second group of colonists who fled to the eastern shores of Maryland and Virginia; he may have gone west with the westward exodus of Lenape natives; or he may have traveled northwest with several Swedish families moving up along the Schuylkill River, which was the farthest away from the slave-holding Dutch and English settlements. My reasoning here is based on the fact that he was last seen and documented as being in New Sweden in 1654 at the Company store gathering supplies.

2. On the other hand, one of the more dire possibilities is that he was taken back into slavery. With slaves moving into the area from the Dutch in the North and the English colonies in the South, he was (needless to say) "hemmed in." Furthermore, with the value of slaves increasing due to the colonies' greater need and the slaves' greater cost, he was now a valuable commodity in more than one sense.

3. Even though it may sound like a long shot, there is a possibility that he boarded or stowed away on a Dutch ship bound for the Spanish Caribbean in hopes of getting back amongst his own people or the area from which he was taken. As unlikely as it may sound, it is a fact that Portuguese and Spanish plantation owners were more considerate of their slaves than the Dutch or English slave owners when it came to manumission. In addition, Anthony would have been able to return to the sea from where he undoubtedly was taken in the beginning of his New Sweden saga.

4. Coming back to a previous point of Anthony escaping to the western interior of Maryland or Pennsylvania with the west-

ward-moving Lenape tribes, this is based on his familiarity with these tribes and their sachems (chiefs). This familiarity would have sprung from his frequent visits to their villages as skipper of Governor Printz' sloop and as his man Friday, who had to make frequent visits during the time period in which no Swedish ships had come with fresh supplies or items to trade. Who knows? He may have begun a romance or mutual relationship with one of the Lenape or other Native American squaws.

5. Finally, he may have died from the sickness and disease that killed so many aboard ship *Orn* (*Eagle*) that brought Johan Classon Risingh, who came to replace Governor Printz. According to Risingh's journal, 230 of the 350 passengers on board had become "sicken" from dysentery and fever a month before landing at Fort Casimir on May 22, 1654. Many of the sick died at sea and their bodies were thrown overboard.

6. The other very real possibility is that he died by other means or he was killed.[17]

A GLIMMER OF HOPE

Now that we know that Anthony was not the only African in and around New Sweden during those early years of the settlement, I will begin to look at the kind of lives those Africans (nearly all men) lived while fulfilling their role as servants or slaves. Very few African women were a part of those first shiploads of slaves brought here aboard Dutch ships because women were not initially used in the fields or as laborers outdoors, the most needed areas for slave labor. Instead, women were used primarily in the households of government and Company officials. Moreover, African men were the "seasoned" population of slaves brought from other Dutch colonies in South America and the southern waters of the Caribbean.

These early groups of African natives came to the colonies in somewhat the same way as their European counterparts—as indentured servants. Both had contracts to serve for a given number of years, although the contract for Africans was not as specific as that of Europeans, nor was it a written document. Most agreements between slave owners and their African slaves were verbal and usually issued after a length of time had passed between the start of the slave's service and the date he or she was promised freedom.

In many ways, however, the servile groups of mostly men who came to these shores during the mid-to-late 17th century weathered the conditions of slavery much better than their descendants and those who came aboard specially designed slave ships that maximized their ability to transport the largest number of human cargo as possible. Those small initial groups of slaves brought in by the Dutch, mostly as booty from raids upon Spanish and Portuguese ships, then later as captives or the result of trading with African chieftains along Africa's west coast (primarily Angola) by novice slave traders, benefited from a life with basic rights and the ability to move from slave-servant to freedman as indicated in the passage below:

> *Slavery under the Dutch, and particularly for those slaves owned by the company, was far more 'benign' during the 40 years [1624 – 1664] they controlled New Netherland than the subsequent period under the English. Bondsmen owned by the company had basic rights. They were admitted to the Dutch Reformed Church and were married by its ministers. Their children were baptized. Slave families were kept together. They could testify in court, sign legal documents, and bring civil actions against whites. A slave was permitted to work after hours, and he was paid on a scale equal to that of white workers. The company built a hospital in New Amsterdam for soldiers and slaves in 1660. Company slaves were promised their freedom in return for faithful service. In 1664, 11 slaves petitioned for and received their freedom; their wives were also freed, and they were given plots of land to work for their support.[18]*

Even among the English, slaves who had been baptized or had accepted and practiced the Christian faith were given the opportunity of freedom. This form of manumission was a result of the prohibition against the enslavement of Christians imposed by the British Crown. Furthermore, children born from enslaved mothers but who had freedman fathers were considered free under Dutch and British law during Anthony's time. This quickly changed after the British took control of all Dutch territories.

What remained as another glimmer of hope for most Africans brought to the New World was the initial reluctance of most Europeans, particularly those who had come for religious freedom, to accept the conditions of "servant for life" assigned to these servants. All Europeans (with little or no exceptions) understood and accepted the system of indentures and many accepted the category of "property" for Africans who did not practice (in their opinion) a Christian way of life, but the notion of making a human being a servant for life was difficult to justify. In New Sweden there were neither the resources nor the desire among Swedish, Finnish and German settlers to acquire slaves from the Dutch. In fact, those few Dutch settlers who did use the services of African laborers did so on a lease from the Dutch West India Company which owned all of the Africans brought to the area.

> *After four years of total control of all activities in the colony by the company, with resulting financial reverses, the policy was changed to allow individuals to develop the settlements. Company slaves were leased to the settlers as well as to the local governments.*[19]

Since a large segment of the population was convinced eventually that Africans were not the same as white servants, making them "servants for life" was not unjustified. On the other hand, a small but persistent group of Quakers, Mennonites and Swedes began a movement that culminated in an official act of protest against slavery in 1688 that led ultimately to the end of slavery and its brutal and inhumane treatment of Africans as other than human beings.[20] Starting in 1648 when the Dutch West India Company began selling its slave cargo and staples rather than using them in their settlements, slave ownership began to take root among the settlers. Settlers of all backgrounds became increasingly possessive of their bondsmen and took every precaution to safeguard their investment. Moreover, they added to their numbers in ways that were not always legal or moral. This fact alone was enough to spur the anti-slavery movement and the end of slavery; in fact, it gave birth to the abolitionist movement and became a precursor of the Underground Railroad. Long before there was a movement, a safe-haven practice or resistance to slavery known as "abolition," there was a scattered collection of Swedes, Quakers and Mennonites who felt that it was their moral and religious duty to help those in lifetime bondage who sought their help to escape that bondage.[21]

This help that was given to runaways and fugitives was very informal and (at times) even self-serving. If a man was a fugitive, the kind of help he could receive would have depended greatly on the reason for his escape from authority and his general character. He could be given the choice to work around the farmstead or mill in exchange for asylum for a limited period of time; or he would have been referred to a more distant location of settlers who could keep him out of the reach of the law in exchange for his service. On the other hand, if the man or woman was a runaway, normally these God-conscious settlers would offer them an open invitation to stay with them to live and work as one of the family. Generally, these runaways were artisans, river workers, and other skilled workers who spoke and understood the language of the Europeans well enough to communicate.[22] The only exception to this generous and neighborly offer would have been the likelihood of being discovered by "slave chasers" very early after their escape. If the settler suspected a visit from a slave chaser based on reports that one was in the area, he would direct the runaway slave to a farther and more secluded location.

Priot to 1664, many of these African fugitives, truants and run-aways chose to stay hidden in households far from well-travelled roads and waterways. It was this clandestine existence by many enslaved Africans that made them invisible to Swedish record-keeping and journals, and therefore, ignored in reports to Company and government officials. After all, if it was reported that a colonist had a servant who was working for him that he did not bring to the colony, or that was not given to him by the Company or purchased by rightful means, he would have to relinquish said servant to the local government officials and face possible fines and penalties for harboring a runaway slave or servant. By the same rights, if a local community of settlers (in this case Swedish) acquired African servants without the knowledge of the South Company or the Swedish government, not only would it have been a violation of the set of instructions given to both Johan Printz and Johan Risingh (Swedish spelling), but also subject to scrutiny by both the Dutch and English trading companies and their governments, which maintained the largest slave population in the area.

After 1664 when England took control of the entire Delaware River Valley and practically the entire East Coast of what is now America, more and more Africans were brought into the area, especially into the areas of Philadelphia and southeastern Delaware. As English settlers moved into the area, the population of Quakers began to rise almost proportionally. That proportional rise was due to the large segment of the new English settlers who were Quakers. Along with the Quakers there was also a noticeable increase in the Mennonite community. Both of these religious communities began a quiet yet persistent protest against the increase in chattel slavery and its lifetime servitude commitment.[23]

Yet the German-Dutch settlers refused to buy slaves themselves and quickly saw the contradiction in the slave trade and in farmers who forced people to work. Although in their native Germany and Holland the Krefelders had been persecuted be-

cause of their beliefs, only people who had been convicted of a crime could be forced to work in servitude. In what turned out to be a revolutionary leap of insight, the Germantowners saw a fundamental similarity between the right to be free from persecution on account of their beliefs and the right to be free from being forced to work against their will.[24]

And in the background of all of that stood the freedom-loving Swede and Finn, whose love for the pristine beauty of the wilderness was surpassed only by their passion for personal freedoms, hard work and personal success.

Unlike the social duty Dutch and English settlers felt to return runaway slaves who would come to their doors, Swedish and Finnish settlers rarely turned over runaways to slave chasers. Just as in later years when many slaves knew where to go to seek freedom, so it was during this early time. Slaves from Virginia and Maryland would travel to the land along the Schuylkill River to live amongst the Swedes, Finns, Quakers and Mennonites for protection, then later travel to Philadelphia where the largest population of free Africans lived. This practice forced many Swedish enclaves to work and live outside the social mainstream of colonial life and to move farther away from its commercial hubs. History has not seen fit to credit the unassuming and unselfish acts of these colonial Nordic people with the first conscious acts of abolition—deliberately helping slaves of lifetime servitude escape that fate.

IT WAS ALL ABOUT THE PROFIT

All through this book I have talked about European and African servants, African slaves, Europeans of economic means and the social conflict that occurred as a result of those different ethnic, religious and economic groups meeting. The unique and disturbing social aspects of this topic have more to do with "why" it happened than with "who" was making it happen or "whom" it was happening to. Stated more simply, the players did not make the scene; it was the scene—the chain of events—that made the players. All through history, various tribal and communal groups contended with one another over having more—more of whatever was prized and precious to the people of that time. So, not unlike any other previous generation of people, those of the 17th century in colonial North America acted upon an age-old human emotional flaw—the need to always have more no matter the consequences. In this case, the level of human civilized sophistication had begun to have a slow worldwide impact on how mankind should treat one another.

No longer were countries, continents, and cultural societies separated and apart from one another. The bold exploration of adventurers and sailors had brought together many different ethnic, racial, cultural, and religious groups in a way that recorded history had not known before on such a wide scale. And, as it has been throughout history, the strong will always seek to subdue and victimize the weak. Stronger Native American tribes were overpowering weaker ones; Europeans were overpowering Native American tribes and taking their lands; stronger European nations were overpowering weaker European nations; and all European nations with the exception of Sweden (at that time) were forcing servitude on aboriginal people in all traveled parts of the world, especially in Africa and the Caribbean Islands.

The way that this greed manifested itself in the early stages of the African slave trade was through taking from others, not trading with others. First, the Portuguese kidnapped Africans from the west coast of Africa; then the Spaniards pirated Africans from the ship decks of Portuguese vessels; after that, Africans were stolen from Spanish ships by the Dutch. The Dutch were so proficient at pirating Spanish and Portuguese ships that they made it into an enterprise, with the best-known of those enterprises being the Dutch West India Company:

> *"While the company had been nominally chartered to trade with and colonize the New Netherland, the real object of its chiefs, had been a colossal system of legalized piracy against the com-*

merce of Spain and Portugal, in Africa and America. ...It had preyed upon Spanish fleets from one side of the Atlantic to the other. It had in two years taken one hundred and four prizes. It frequently sent out squadrons of seventy armed vessels to sweep the seas. ...It had declared dividends of fifty percent. These spectacularly and enormously profitable performances had dazzled the wealth-worshipping Dutch mind and completely cast into the shade the humble profits of plodding..."[25]

Even though much has been written of this "period of exploration," little has been recorded or admitted in most historical contexts that reveals the real motivation for the imperialistic and empire-building mentality of coastal European countries. It was a sinister game of "one-upmanship" and a treacherous game of "imperialistic leapfrog." This was a period of acquiring wealth and riches at the expense of others, not with the help of others. By understanding the psychological motivations of this period, it becomes much easier to understand the push for profits over the push for human dignity.

When the Spanish came to North America, the Africans they brought with them were used by them for their service. They did not make a market for them to others. Likewise, the Dutch as they began building New Netherland brought Africans in as the labor force, not as a marketable commodity. Then, there was that conscious shift away from an "outpost/trading post" company focus, to one of "community building" and "new world building" company focus, which brought about a social paradigm shift that this country (and much of the world) still wrestles with. When the Dutch West India Company turned its attention to the profit of trading in human cargo, all of the major colonizing countries in North America became active participants, except for Sweden. Even though Sweden did not become an active participant in the slave trade during the late 1600s and the majority of the 1700s, the lure of the vast wealth being gained from this worldwide trade brought Sweden into it as a middleman and parts supplier for slavers.[26]

This was, perhaps, the first time in recorded history that a worldwide activity (other than war) was able to create a profitable niche for vast numbers of small enterprises. Even though the risks both in acquiring and transporting Africans were high, the prospect of profitable returns as high as 50% outweighed those risks.[27] In spite of this fact, individual Swedes and Finns, as a norm, did not invest in this growing and legitimizing of the slave trade. Instead, many began a crusade of "non-involvement" helping (on a very small scale) only those who happened to cross their paths. That effort and many similar uncoordinated acts were greatly overshadowed by the actions of profit-driven European companies and their governments, which provided slaves to the colony.

In the following chapters of this book, you will be presented with many historical facts that differed from primary source facts which will actually tell the story of the Africans' role in 17th century New Sweden and the Delaware River Valley. Along with these facts will be fortuitous and deliberate inferences that will challenge you to weigh the measure of inferred fact against historical redundancies. In more frank terms, you will read many passages in my book that have not graced the pages of mainstream academia and which will challenge you to give more thought than what is usually required. Bear this in mind as you continue to delve into the heart of this untold saga.

CHAPTER FIVE

The Dutch Influence on Africans in New Sweden

THE COMPANY COLONY AND THE CITY COLONY

One of the most significant changes to the Dutch empire in North America took place after the conquest of New Sweden in 1655. The Dutch West India Company, in debt to the City of Amsterdam for financing the conquest of New Sweden, made a quick bargain with the City to sell land that they held along the Delaware River running from the Christina River to Bombay Hook. This deal for the City to purchase a colony in America was the first and last time in recorded history that a European city, or any city for that matter, has ever taken ownership of an American colony.[1] This in-house land deal between these two divergent Dutch governing bodies divided the Dutch empire in North America into two very distinct areas that helped open up a significant wave of slave importation to Delaware.

> *When the new colonists sent by the city of Amsterdam arrived at New Amstel in the spring of 1657 they found only twenty families, mostly Swedes, settled around the old Dutch fort. With the coming of this expedition, the settlements on the Delaware were divided into two colonies. Below the Christina River, centered on New Amstel (modern New Castle) was the colony administered by the city of Amsterdam, sometimes referred to by the name of*

its chief town. With the arrival of the 150 people of the city's first expedition, this "City Colony" became predominantly Dutch.

North of the Christina River lay a second colony, predominantly Swedish and Finnish in population, still administered by the Dutch West India Company. Isolated from New Amsterdam by the unsettled wilderness of New Jersey, this "Company Colony" was administered by a deputy appointed by Stuyvesant who made old Fort Christina, now called Altena, his headquarters.²

More and more slaves were brought to both areas in order to complete the necessary transformation from a colony based on export of beaver pelts and other animal furs and sustained by the commercial company, to a more self-sufficient and self-sustaining colony based on agricultural productivity.³ In addition to the labor needed to increase the agricultural production, there was also the increased labor needed to clear forests and to harvest pine and oak trees used in shipbuilding because waterways were still the most convenient and affordable way to move goods and people in the Delaware River valley.⁴ Even though very little information was recorded about this, Africans were brought to New Netherland not only to perform menial and arduous tasks, but also to help defend and spearhead attacks against Native Americans.

Revenge was considered necessary to offer security to the lives of the settlers and their cattle. Fast-running blacks with swords and half-lances were to lead the attack.⁵

To defend the settlement, local officials turned to black people, and often rewarded them with grants of freedom and land.

Black men had long been called to the service of the colony. They were regularly armed and they served in the militia. Earlier, when tenants near Beverwijick refused to pay quitrents to patron Kiliaen Van Rensselaer, the schout (sheriff) of the manor used slaves 'as brute forces against the malevolent.' ...'the strongest and most active of the negroes as can conveniently [be]

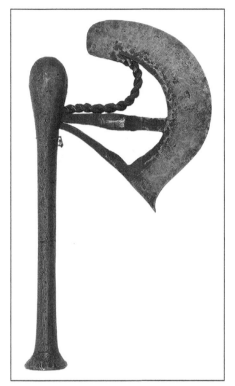

This is the African nzappa zap (also known as zappozap or ka-suyu), which is a traditional African weapon similar to an axe or hatchet. It has an ornate wrought-iron blade connected to a club-like wooden handle, often clad in copper, bronze or brass. In practice, it is used much like the American tomahawk, both thrown for short distances and as a melee weapon in hand-to-hand combat. It differs from the usual axe style, in that the blade mounts to looping prongs that affix to the shaft.

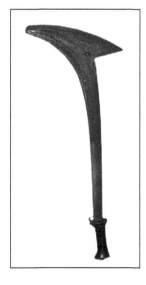

African Gbaya. A traditional weapon found in the villages of Cameroon, for many years used as both a weapon and an agricultural tool favored by warriors. The shape of the blade is based on the head of a bird, complete with a copper rivet for an eye.

spare[d] and provide[d] them with a small ax and half-pike' to protect the Dutch enclave.[6]

As the Dutch moved from the Hudson River Valley (where threats against the colony were more frequent) into other areas along the Delaware River, these trained African warriors were always there to scout the areas and to help establish a defense perimeter.

> *And the Dutch in New Amsterdam in 1641 aimed to use the strongest and fleetest Negroes to fight Indians with hatchets and half-pike. Governor Pieter Stuyvesant in 1658 requested that the Dutch West India Company send 'clever and strong Negroes' to work and to fight Native Americans, either directly or as adjuncts in carrying supplies.*[7]

Having lived peacefully with the newly arrived Swedes, Finns and peaceful Dutch Mennonites and Quakers, the Lenape, Nanticoke, Choptank and other Native American tribes along the Delaware and Chesapeake did not pose the same hostilities as their Minqua and Iroquois cousins to the north.[8]

As a result, many of these sentinel/combat-readied Africans were shifted to other duties or were rewarded with their freedom and became part of the free African population that existed during Anthony Swart's time and the time of the New Sweden colony. Unfortunately, since very little information is available on this topic, detailed facts and numbers cannot be given at this time. On the other hand, it can be inferred that some were drafted into the service of rounding up runaway servants, which was having a noticeable effect on the worker shortage in the City Colony that now had to procure their own slaves.

Prior to the Dutch takeover of New Sweden, all African slaves were provided to areas of the Dutch colonies by the Dutch West India Company, which was now the Company Colony. As I have mentioned previously, slaves brought to New Netherland were brought by Dutch privateers who kidnapped African slaves from Spanish and Portuguese vessels, or they were brought up by company ships from their plantations in Brazil or Curacao. Both of these methods of obtaining slave labor were too slow and too little to meet the growing need for additional labor in North America, particularly in the City Colony. Furthermore, the company's policy of leasing these servants to settlers and government officials had become too costly for the company to continue. As a result, Dutch slave

A Lenape family
(Courtesy of the Delaware Public Archives)

traders were instructed to bring shiploads of Africans from Africa directly to New Amsterdam where they were sold to Dutch as well as English settlers in dire need of their labor.

In a few instances, small shipments of Africans had already been brought to English colonies at Jamestown in 1619 and Massachusetts as early as 1624. In fact, 20 male Africans were brought from a Dutch man-of-war ship in exchange for food, which the ship's crew was in dire need of.[9]

What began as an answer to a severe labor shortage soon became one of the most profitable worldwide-based commercial enterprises the world has ever seen—and the most nefarious. What began as only a trickle (comparatively speaking) soon became a gushing torrent of commercial trade in human misery. Some of that trade that landed on these shores set in motion a social phenomenon that cascaded in

Carrying provisions for the village.
(Courtesy of the Delaware Public Archives)

different directions. New Amsterdam (present-day New York City) became the center for that trade for the Company Colony but later steered clear of profiting from free labor to profiting from the sales of free labor[10]. On the other hand, New Amstel (present-day New Castle) became a center for that trade for all points south of the Christina River, which may help explain the lack of a "slavery buffer zone"[11] in years to come.

Nearly all of southern Delaware (below what is now the Chesapeake and Delaware Canal—C & D Canal) was populated by Dutch farmers of the City Colony (who had slaves) and the English farmers from Maryland and Virginia who brought slaves with them. What I also found that was quite surprising, yet not unique to the Delaware

Indian types (front & back positions).
(Courtesy of the Delaware Public Archives)

colony, was the number of indentured servants who left New Netherland after serving their term of servitude to settle farther south in
Maryland and Virginia to start small farmsteads. These small farmers
could only afford one or two slaves at most, and they were forced to
keep them for as long as possible. In fact, the first incident of dealing with runaway slaves in this region came from the complaint of a
small farmer, not a large plantation owner.[12]

The harsh treatment experienced by many former indentured
servants led to similar treatment of their slaves, most notably by the
English. The English settler's view of slavery was different from that
held by the other European colonists in the area and led to increased
incidents of runaways, insurrections and slave revolts. An English in-

Religious celebrations.
(Courtesy of the Delaware Public Archives)

dentured servant was historically and habitually treated harshly and with little regard to his "rights" as an Englishman. He was completely under the control of his master. He could not raise his hand against his master, and he had to seek his master's permission to marry, engage in a trade, buy whiskey, or leave the plantation. Furthermore, an English servant could not vote or hold any type of office in the colony. Longing to escape such restrictions, white servants were frequent runaways, which instigated black servants and slaves to run away too.[13]

Contrary to widely held historical accounts, the claim that there were significant increases in the African slave population in the Dutch-held territory that is now Delaware after the English victory in 1664 is without merit. The slave population in the area actually leveled off and, in and around New Castle, even slipped downward. Why? Because English officers confiscated all of the Dutch slaves and sold or bartered them to Maryland and Virginia planters in order to get much-needed food and supplies.[13a]The population that did increase directly following England's dominance of the East Coast was that of English servants. The African slave population did not increase significantly until the 1690s, when English masters had had enough of the difficulties holding onto white servants.[14]

Another event that affected slave population growth after the English victory was the large population of Swedish and Finnish homesteads that remained intact almost as they were. Even though New Sweden as a colony no longer existed after the English takeover, they were given a great deal of autonomy and remained known as the Swedish Nation. This was possible due to the generous surrender terms afforded to them by the Dutch, then later the English:

> *The surrender terms were more generous than the residents had reasons to expect from an invading force. The Dutch, Swedish, Finnish, and other alien farmers and craftsmen were allowed to retain their homes and personal property. Those who did not want to live under the Duke of York's rule were free to depart unmolested and to take their personal property with them.*[15]

Delaware Tribes gather.

As was their culture and social norm, they did not encourage nor participate in the use of slaves to do the homestead and farming work they themselves were accustomed to doing. By granting them rights to self-rule in many areas, the English not only allowed for this community to have a definitive role in the shaping of this region, but also the acknowledgement of them as a respectable governing body—ergo, the Swedish Nation, which began under the Dutch.

AFRICANS REPLACE NATIVE AMERICANS IN THE FIELDS

When the Spaniards first began conquering the islands of the Caribbean, the natives on those islands were forced to work the gold and silver mines, then later the large plantations. Huge populations of natives died from disease, sickness and molestation at the hands of their captives.[16] In addition to those who died were those who ran away and established bands of renegade groups.

Based on that experience, it was recommended by a monk, Bartolomeo de las Casas (Protector of the Indians) that Africans replace the Indians as the primary labor force.[17] His reasoning for this shift in the labor force was based on the Africans' ability to work well in the tropical weather and conditions of the islands and their stronger immunity to diseases,[18] which were decimating the Indian population on the islands. [18a] Furthermore, the physical differences in Africans from that of the European and Indian population and their unfamiliarity with the terrain made it harder for them to escape from the plantations. Thus began Europe's most concerted claim to Africans taken from the continent to work the fields of Caribbean Islands, South America, and then Central and North America.

Native American chieftains.
(Courtesy of the Delaware Public Archives)

With so many colonies in close proximity to each other and the need for large numbers of laborers, Spaniards (in particular) were using more and more aboriginal tribes in Central and North America, but not in native homelands. What they had learned from their experiences in the Caribbean was that exporting the natives from their areas of familiarity to unfamiliar areas reduced the risks of escape and the creation of marauding groups of insurgents or "maroons" as they became known.[19] Nevertheless, there were several Spanish colonies in what is now Florida that forgot to apply those labor transfer rules and lost large numbers of soldiers and settlers as a result of trying to impose forced labor on the local tribes. [19a]

With far too few white indentured servants to serve the needs of the ambitious New Sweden settlement, Johan Printz, New Sweden's first royal governor, attempted (contrary to his Official Instructions) to place Delaware Indians into his forced labor workforce. After all, the governor had a most difficult and almost insurmountable task to perform per his Official Instructions. He had been given a mandate to settle lands along both sides of the Delaware that extended from the Schuylkill River to the north all the way to Duck Creek

Native Americans being enslaved by the Spanish, 1596

to the south.[20] It is probably fair to say that Printz based his decision to use the Lenape, or "original people," as forced workers due to their peaceable nature and their village life that included farming, fishing and hunting. Another determining factor could have been the ready availability of war captives—Native Americans who were made slaves as a consequence of captivity. Needless to say, this was a failed attempt that nearly cost Governor Printz much-needed alliances with neighboring tribes. He attempted to use male Indians to clear forests, work farmlands, tend to livestock and grind corn and barley. These were duties performed by the women of Native American tribes, not by the men. This was seen as a serious insult not only to those who were taken and forced to work but also to those who felt threatened by those actions.

With few items to use as trade due to the long period of isolation from Mother Sweden, Printz was forced to use bluffing tactics to force his will with neighboring tribes which had threatened New

Sweden's normal period of calm and safety. If it had not been for the encroachment of the Dutch and English into the area, which the Lenapes favored much less, Printz would have surely undermined the continued establishment of New Sweden and the Swedish Nation.

As I pointed out earlier, there was little or no chance of keeping the Indians of the Delaware River Valley captive on a settlement in the midst of their own native grounds. Besides Native Americans who were war captives and sold or traded to Europeans by warring tribes, enslaved Native Americans in service to Europeans rarely remained obedient or confined to the settlement for very long. The only exceptions to this pattern were the Native American women and children under 18, who were preferred over Africans in the European farmstead. In addition, runaway natives could rarely be brought back to the settlement because it was too difficult to recognize and identify them, too much of a risk of reprisal from local tribes, and too much of an expense to hunt for them. Although the exact number of Native Americans and aboriginal people from the islands of the Caribbean and South America is not known, it is fair to estimate that the number of enslaved Indians was in the tens of thousands. The majority were natives transferred from North America to the plantations in the Caribbean and vice versa.[21] The two-way travel of this type of trading proved itself too expensive for all of the European colonizers, with the exception of the Dutch and the Spanish, who were the leading slave traders until the British conquered the Dutch in 1664.

What appeared to be a logical and financially prudent transformation of the English labor force and substitution of Africans for Native Americans on the plantations and in the fields was anything but logical, prudent or reasonable. In short, it was simply a matter of racial prejudice and forced circumstances. It was, by far, easier to explain to religious-minded Europeans why Africans had to be enslaved than it was to explain the enslavement of a people who preceded them to this very land. It was easier to catch and return a runaway Negro slave than a homegrown Native American. And it was, by far, easier to "season" (train in language and work manner) a black African in this unknown land than it was to "season" the natives. By and large, forced circumstances brought on by widespread deaths of male Native Americans from European diseases and intermarriage of Africans with Native Americans and white female servants played definitive roles in this calculated labor transition.

The shared history of vicious and abusive treatment of all servants at the hands of their English masters further intensified the need for changes in the fields. No longer would white masters allow white servants or Native American slaves to work alongside Africans for fear of an alliance that would breed pockets of insurrection and hostilities, which aided Africans more than it did whites and Native American servants. Regrettably, English slave masters watched almost helplessly as more and more indentured Europeans fanned the flames of revolt and hostilities in the midst of angry and confused Africans. For most owners, separating them still was not enough, because the cross-culture bonds from the shared life of captivity created an angry underclass comparable to the coalition of poor whites, African Americans and Latinos of modern times. Consequently, as an added protection against such unholy alliances, they gave common Englishmen more power and rights over Africans to assure their duplicity in the maintenance of this chattel slave society.

AFRICANS POPULATE THE COLONY

Even though Sweden's ambitious goal of settling all of the area along the Delaware or South River and Bay fell short of its goal thanks to the aggressive actions of Peter Stuyvesant, Swedish and Finnish countrymen continued to greatly influence the entire region well into the early 18th century. Collectively, they were no longer known as New Sweden but instead, due to their socio-economic impact upon farming and grist mills and their retention of important and strategic political positions under the Dutch and the English, they continued to exist as a very influential component known as the Swedish Nation. This influence initially helped to slow and impede the increasing numbers of Africans that were brought to the area.[22] This zero growth in the slave population was due in part to the Swedish and Finnish social order and work ethics and to the initial desire of the English to bring more indentured countrymen to help populate and settle their newly acquired fertile lands. However, that situation soon gave way to the harsh reality of the increased production of a very labor-intensive crop, which needed many more workers than those coming in long-awaited ships from England.

By the 1680s, the English had begun to take over the Dutch slave trade on the West Coast of Africa but still needed Dutch captains to navigate into certain parts of the African coastline to initiate slave trades. In addition, English vessels were intercepting Dutch ships bound for plantations in the West Indies and on the northern coast of South America in order to capture their slave cargo. The combined effort of bringing shiploads of Africans to the East Coast plantations of Maryland and Virginia and more Maryland and Virginia slave owners relocating to the fertile soil of the Delaware coastline began a new wave of African presence in the Delaware River Valley.[23] Unlike the small groups of Africans brought in by the Dutch to help the growth of small farmsteads by clearing forests and building forts and ships, these were large groups of Africans shipped in to work, mostly, tobacco plantations. Slaves were brought not only to English plantation owners but also to open slave markets to be sold to the highest bidder. It was this open slave market, the epicenter of the African Diaspora in North America, that changed all aspects of colonial and societal America from that time forth. Adding to the steady rise in the slave population was the increase in the number of female slaves and the enactment of laws guaranteeing that children of slave mothers would remain as slaves, regardless of the father's status. Those changes, along with the steady flow of new slave owners to the area soon to be known as Delaware, created a slave population explosion that later required legislative action to control the numbers.[24]

In addition to significant numbers of slaves that were brought to the lower counties—areas around Whorekill or Hoerenkil (present day Lewes) and south to the Maryland boundary—there were also shiploads brought to the Philadelphia area by merchants, shipbuilders and factory owners. Records indicated that there were 150 Africans brought to Philadelphia aboard the British merchant ship *Isabella* in 1684,[25] which began a steady flow of this form of cheap labor to a growing mercantile English colony. More importantly, after William Penn's land grant from the Duke of York in 1680 there began a steady stream of Quakers moving into that same area, which brought and accepted large numbers of African slaves. In fact, the Quaker community was so hungry for slaves that they soon held a larger share of the slave population than their meager numbers could justify.[26] By 1693, Africans were so numerous in the colony's capital that the Philadelphia Council complained of "the tumultuous gatherings of the Negroes in the town of Philadelphia." By the turn of the century, one out of every ten Philadelphians owned a slave, while one in fifteen families in Pennsylvania owned one or more slaves.[27] As families and businesses moved from the cramped areas of this bustling city on the rise to more spacious livable areas in the Three Lower Counties (now the state of Delaware), they, like those from Maryland, came with their slaves. Those combined migratory movements not only brought larger numbers of Africans to what is now Delaware than what had existed, but also branded the state with its unique societal bipolar condition regarding the institution of slavery and African Americans—the social order and conscientiousness of "the northernmost county in Mississippi" as well as that of the states to its north.[28] At this point it should be clear how and why Africans began to populate this once nearly slave-free Swedish colony.

CHAPTER SIX

The English Influence
on Swedish Settlers

MARYLAND ENGLISH FARMERS BRING SLAVE LIFE TO DELAWARE

Africans were brought to the City Colony (Lower Delaware) not only by Dutch slave ships, but also by Maryland and Virginia planters seeking to benefit from the richness of Delaware's fertile and mostly virgin farmlands. This migration of English landowners created a small but steady flow of Africans and white indentured servants to Delaware, reaching proportions after 1660 that soon gave rise to serious concerns about the institution of slavery that did not exist previously under the rule of the Dutch or the Swedes:

> *Although the demand for slaves always exceeded the supply, the number imported by the Dutch never reached such proportions as to cause serious apprehension or difficulty during the period of their domination.*[1]

In fact, after the English claimed all Dutch-held territories in North America in 1664, the character and the scope of the institution of slavery changed. This change not only affected the treatment of African slaves, but also white indentured servants, who were being brought in large numbers to these newly-expanding English colonies. With few opportunities available to them in England, some 70% to 85% of colonists from England came as "indentures." They worked alongside African slaves and often received the same harsh treatment dispensed to Africans. Such treatment of their fellow Englishmen created hostile and rebellious groups of whites and Africans that restricted the importation of new Africans to the area, at least until calmer tempers prevailed.[2]

During this period, white servants began to realize that they had more in common with black servants than they did with their white owners.[3] Before this shared social intimacy between black and white servants was confronted, large English landowners and the colonial governments denied that any such alliance between the two groups existed. Instead of working to end the resentment among white and black laborers and small farmers, they instituted practices that were intended to separate the two groups. However, it made white servants more resentful and restless. The rebellions and uprisings that resulted from large groups of restless, poor white men convinced plantation owners to rethink their use of white men for labor versus African slaves.[4]

One incident in particular that occurred in Virginia in 1676 was the Bacon Rebellion. It was led by Nathaniel Bacon, a 29-year-old English farmer, who had recently arrived in the Virginia colony but had been there long enough to experience and witness the harsh and insensitive attitudes of plantation owners and the royal governor, Sir William Berkeley. Bacon was able to galvanize a group of black slaves, white indentured servants, and small farmers to rebel against the government's failure to protect them against repeated Indian raids. Due to Bacon's sudden death from dysentery during the uprising, the rebellion failed, but the alliance of blacks and poor whites succeeded in changing the attitudes of the government and plantation owners which, unfortunately, favored poor whites, but not black slaves.[5]

Fearing the worst if those hostilities escalated, many white indentures were not only released from bonded service, but also given their own land to farm, thus increasing the number of white farmers capable of owning black African slaves. Furthermore, the Colonial government working in tandem with wealthy landowners conspired

Battle scene from the Bacon Rebellion of 1676

to make certain that white men would not desire future allegiance with black slaves by making the least of them superior to all black slaves. In my opinion, the generosity and leniency extended to white servants, coupled with harsh and restrictive laws placed on Africans (both free and bonded) as a result of this rebellion, efficaciously marked the beginning of institutionalized racism, characterized as racial slavery.[6] The release of white servants from indentures with land to farm and the increase of English settlers and convict servants coming directly from England to start a farmstead or plantation resulted in larger populations of planters that began to directly affect Swedish and Finnish farmers. They were seeing not only more and more rich farm areas being gobbled up by Englishmen, but also an increase in the use of slaves as the primary labor force on those English farms and plantations. A few Swedish households opportunistically made use of slaves that they claimed were runaways, thus avoiding any suspicion of owning a slave.

As the number of Africans began its steady increase in the late 17th century, white English landowners (particularly plantation owners) became threatened by what they feared would result from their ill treatment of white servants and African slaves. As mentioned previously in this text, many white indentured servants served and worked right alongside Native Americans and African slaves. This co-existence—working together in the fields and homes of the master and living together in communal living quarters—created not only an angry sub-class in the English colony but also a new social class of mulattos, creoles and mixed-breeds of Native Americans and Africans, which necessitated more restrictive laws to define and differentiate these new groups. Landowners' attempts to contain discontented white servants and Native American slaves on the plantation proved to be too much of a burden. Realizing, instead, the benefit of having a black slave who could be easily recognized and apprehended should he try to escape and, furthermore, could be purchased outright, thus stabilizing an owner's labor supply, plantation owners quickly turned to importation of Africans in large shipments.

In addition to the slaves that Maryland farmers brought to Delaware, they also brought their slavery laws or "black codes," which not only distinguished slave from servant, but also categorized the different types of servants and slaves. They further established legal restrictions on marriage among servants and slaves, as well as determined the legal status of the children born of lawful and unlawful marriages.[7] By far, the infiltration and migration of English farmers from Maryland into lower Delaware had influenced and continued to influence the social, political and economic thinking of that region long after that initial settling. Even though all of the colonies controlled by the English had some type of slave codes (deemed necessary as the population of slaves increased as well as its ratio to whites), by far, according to G. W. Williams,[8] Maryland's black codes were the most restrictive and harshest of all the colonies. Some historians dispute his claim, but only on the premise that all of the black codes appeared to be just as harsh, cruel and inhumane as the next. I maintain that the difference in the harshness of one colony's slave or black codes versus that of another colony would have been the far-reaching consequences of the codes and the quickness and frequency of being enforced.[9]

Having more hindsight and much less prejudicial scrutiny, I strongly support what I have read of the venerable George Washington Williams' accounts of slavery in the colonies of North America. Even though he referred to Virginia as "the mother of slavery," it was not mentioned to imply that it was the worst, but only that it was the first colony to import slaves in 1619.

LIFE IN DELAWARE SURROUNDED BY SLAVERY

One of my questions concerning the disappearance of Black Anthony in 1654 was whether or not he had been taken back into slavery. With populations of black slaves to the north and south of Delaware, there must have been pressure on any black person, regardless of his status, to avoid bounty hunters or slave hunters and others trying to make a quick buck by selling him into slavery. These questionable paralegal individuals (operating most of the time well outside of the law) were introduced by way of several Fugitive Slave Laws, first in New England, then in Virginia and Maryland. This was just another phase in the tightening noose of slavery's rope around the freedoms being denied to Africans in this growing acceptance of the institution of slavery. Donald Wright, in his book, *African Americans in the Colonial Era*, summed up the problems for free Africans in this way:

> *In some ways the existence of slavery hindered free blacks. Slaves who rose to responsible positions under their masters' employ posed no threat to white society, but free blacks who achieved important positions by themselves did. So whites took care to see that northern free black persons [blacks north of the Delaware Bay] remained in menial jobs. Free black shopkeepers had difficulty getting credit; free black artisans were not always welcome*

in shipyards or at building sites. For those who were destitute it was more difficult in freedom than in slavery.[10]

If we apply this explanation to Black Anthony's situation, who was shown in records to be a free man after Johan Printz left the colony, it could be argued that he may have been harassed or victimized by the newcomers brought by Johan Risingh. After all, he was basically in the employ of Governor Johan Printz, who had left his position as governor and also his estate at Tinicum, leaving Anthony on his own. Those same records that indicated his free status did not give reference to his work status or if he had retained any of the responsibilities that he had under Governor Printz. Furthermore, no records had even mentioned his job capacity, citizenship or ownership rights.

As I mentioned earlier, the only inference one can make from what the history and records do show is that Governor Printz abandoned Anthony, even though earlier records showed he was a faithful servant and worker. Even worse, Johan Risingh made no mention of him in any reports or any of the tallies or signatures taken from the settlers. Assuming that Anthony was still in the Colony after Risingh's triumphant arrival, he should have been given some type of recognition for his service and for staying in the Colony, even after his boss had fled. These are just some of the inferences and conjectures that can be made based on the changing social attitudes toward Africans and bonded servants.

As we turn our attention again to those who had turned the life of a free African in Delaware to one of fear and insecurity, based on a high demand for cheap labor among small landowners (the largest segment of English landowners who came to Delaware), we find that selling undocumented Africans as slaves was an easy transaction. The purchase of a bonded African slave as a slave-for-life was a much better deal than accepting indentured white servants with fixed lengths of service, if the price was right. Except for the majority of the Swedish Nation, small-time planters did not question the origin of cheap labor, as long as the price was right. After all, finding cheap labor (preferably slaves to work their fields) was becoming much more difficult after the fall of the Dutch empire in North America, which collapsed the Dutch slave trade. Not only were fewer slaves being brought to these East Coast colonies now under English rule, but also their prized cash crop, tobacco, was losing its value. Ironically, this created a greater rather than a lesser need for cheap labor, because more crops had to be planted to compensate for tobacco's declining value. Forests had to be cleared and fields prepared to plant more and even different crops. To address the problem of declining slave imports, colonial governments turned to domestic ways to create a slave population.

Virginia, the first English colony in America to bring in black Africans to use as slaves in 1619, also became the first to legalize a perpetual system of slavery. This system was created by declaring that black children born would be determined by the mother's status not the father's, as required under English law.[11] This was just another expedient means of dealing with the ever-increasing labor shortage, which was exacerbated by the high number of runaways and truants, and the agonizing cost of replacing them. On the other hand, it created a heinous niche for men looking to cash in on the illicit practice of selling free Africans into slavery.

Emboldened by the wide acceptance of slavery to the north, many of these actions had occurred in Virginia long before slavery had been legalized there in 1660. If you are wondering, as I wondered, why Virginia waited a relatively long period of time to legalize slavery (from 1619–1660), it may have been due to the wide acceptance of the practice. For the most part, prior to large groups of English indentured servants and convict servants coming to these shores in the late 1600s, African and Indian servants were accepted features of that society.

Following Virginia's lead, Maryland legalized slavery and wasted no time in imposing harsher and more drastic provisions to their slave codes than Virginia. These actions taken by Maryland justify my acceptance of Dr. G. W. Williams' claim that Maryland had the harshest slave codes. Additionally, I believe Maryland imposed these harsh codes to keep runaways from using their colony as a safe haven.

During the 1660s, Delaware was experiencing a slow but steady influx of African slaves that had been brought in by the Dutch of New Netherland and the newly-arriving English landowners from the Bay shores of Maryland and Virginia in the late 1660s.

> *I solicite [sic] most seriously that it may please your honor [Peter Stuyvesant] to accommodate me with a company of negroes, as I am very much in want of them in many respects.*
>
> VICE DIRECTOR WILLIAM BECKMAN,
> ALTENA (FORT CHRISTINA), 1662[12]

> *Most Eastern Shore gentry were able to survive the economic hard times of the late seventeenth and the first decade of the eighteenth century, but many of the 'middling and lesser sorts' found that falling tobacco prices left them no alternative except to leave the developed areas at home to take advantage of the liberal land policies that characterized the west bank of the Delaware. Because these migrants of limited means usually did not own slaves, they brought only a few blacks with them.*[13]

Delaware, with its rich soil for agriculture and its numerous swift-moving rivers and streams as a power source for early mills and convenient transportation routes, was fast becoming a very desirable colony for settlers. In fact, the new English leadership felt strongly that the failure of the Swedes to use slaves in their colony is what caused their colony to fail. The combined efforts of the Duke of York's government and that of William Penn's government established attractive policies to bring pro-slavery-minded settlers to Delaware:

> *To attract new immigrants to the west bank [of the Delaware], the duke of York's government established a liberal land-grant policy that caused some Swedes, Finns, and Dutch who were al-*

ready living along the west bank to move inland. This policy also attracted Anglo-Saxon residents of Maryland's Eastern Shore to the unworked soil of present-day central and southern Delaware. Eastern Shore farmers were encouraged to bring their slaves with them when, in 1675, Governor Sir Edmund Andros instructed the high sheriff of the west bank to grant newcomers land in proportion to 'their capacity and number of hands they shall bring for clearing it.' Andros was so interested in giving 'all manner of encouragement to planters of all nations, but especially Englishmen,' that he offered to remit the first three years of quitrents[14] to new settlers. So successful were the combined attractions of virgin soil and the liberal land-grant policies of the duke of York and, after 1682, William Penn, that one source estimates that the population of Delaware increased by more than three times between 1670 and 1700.[15]

The liberal land grants were bringing the pro-slavery-minded landowners, but they were not bringing in the desired amount of slaves. The Dutch West India Company was supplying slaves to the City Colony prior to its capture by the English, but the Duke of York had not assumed any responsibility for doing the same for his proprietors. William Penn and Lord Baltimore were the proprietors of Pennsylvania and Maryland, respectively, and they brought Africans to the Delaware River and Bay area by way of the port cities of Philadelphia and Annapolis. Even though Africans arriving in Delaware from both of these areas were few in number prior to 1700, they still represented a significant increase above the number of Africans known to exist during the time of the Swedish Colony. Furthermore, the largest segment of the English society coming into the area were indentured servants, or in other words, slaves by another name. With that reference point in mind, it is easy to see why I have concluded that life in Delaware after Swedish rule became surrounded by slavery.

CHAPTER SEVEN

African Contributions In and Around the Swedish Settlement: 1639-1700

W hen I started writing this book in 2008, I was very optimistic that I would triumph over all the naysayers who were doubtful that I would find any credible evidence of African contributions during this period of 1639-1700. More specifically, they doubted that I would find that evidence within the Swedish Nation, which had grown far beyond the limited residential area of the original Swedish Colony.

Now, some three-and-a-half years later, I find myself less optimistic, yet still very positive of what I have been able to find. There is no doubt in my mind that there were a number of significant Africans of superior skills who contributed greatly to the evolution of the European business ventures of fishing, fur trading and pirating (the looting activities of privateers) and to that of colonizing.[1]

The establishment of the American colonies' most staple and money-producing crops—tobacco, rice, cotton, corn, indigo and sugar cane—would not have been as profitable as quickly if not for the intervention of skilled Africans with centuries of proven agricultural skills.

In the middle of the 17th century the black population had an enormous impact on colonial life and went through a series of changes that would change the general makeup of the colonies.[2]

Considering the limited amount of references on this topic I have had to work with, and the limited official record or reporting attention any African received—except runaways, truants, maroons, fugitives, and such—my most reliable source has been the advertising for escaped slaves. Slave masters, slave chasers, slave catchers, and local law enforcers of all types spent considerable time and money posting detailed descriptions of valued slaves and servants, because the cost to capture and return them was much less than the time and money already invested in them.

During the mid-to-late-17th century, very descriptive Notices always listed the fugitive's name, talents, physical attributes and character in a humane manner. A few typical 17th-century Notices would read as follows:

> *Prince had Guinea Country marks on his face; Leonard was 40, 5 feet 10 inches [much above normal height for a slave] … can Read & Write …can bleed & draw teeth—£3 reward; He is a blacksmith; has drove a carriage, can shave & dress hair, & is a cobbling shoemaker; Speaks Swede & English well*[3]

In stark contrast to those Notices were the newspaper and poster advertisements for runaways in the mid-to-late-18th century. They listed mutilated body markings such as branded "Rs" on the face, missing ears, severe lash markings to the back and missing male genitals.

In addition, these advertisements would include a master's surname and the reward or punishment for the slave.[4] Contrasting the human value given to slaves in those two different periods offers further proof of the value placed on an individual slave's ability to benefit the colony during the 17th century versus the simple loss of a slave's labor utility during the 18th century. Additionally, 17th-century slave owners had the cost and inconvenience of having to replace the escaped bound servant. Bear in mind that slaves were very few in comparison to indentured servants and other settlers, due to the limited importation of Africans prior to 1700, thus any loss of a slave was costly. Furthermore, manumission of slaves was much more common and a much easier process to pursue than it was after 1700.[5] There was no census taken that recorded an accurate count of the number of free Africans living amongst slaves during this period, but estimates put the number of free Africans between 5-10% of all Africans.

During the 17th century, the runaway problem in Delaware was not slaves leaving this area, but those coming to the area from Maryland and Virginia. I believe the amicable trading relationships of the Swedes and the Dutch with the English from Maryland and Virginia—one based on tobacco, the other on slaves—could have been an enticement, perhaps unknowingly, for slaves to run away to the Delaware Colony in hopes of finding better working conditions and less harshness.[6] The type of slave that escaped to this area would have been capable of concluding that the Delaware Colony did not have very large tobacco and other cash crop plantations requiring back-breaking sunup to sundown work, otherwise the Swedes would not have had to conduct trades for those items. Very able-bodied slaves with language skills, knowledge of maps and of the well-travelled roads and trails were the typical slaves to escape to the land of the Swedes from the plantations or other types of work details of the eastern shores of Maryland and Virginia. Many of those escapees were given refuge by Swedish and Finnish settlers prior to 1670; afterwards, an ever-growing community of Quakers in the southern Pennsylvania colony was added to the list of those giving refuge.

Those Africans who escaped with white indentured servants were often rewarded with gainful employment or subsistence alongside their white counterparts, which is another reason for me to hold to the notion that Africans played a very significant role in the transformation of patchwork European colonies to the birth of a "united" nation. This conviction of mine is further confirmed by statements and views held by those in colonial leadership as early as 1645. The brother-in-law of Governor John Winthrop of Massachusetts upheld

Drawing of runaway slave.

the view that "the colony would never thrive until we get ... a stock of slaves sufficient to do our business."[7] In Delaware, after the Dutch took possession of all Swedish lands and turned their colonizing attention to agriculture and growing cash crops, they too realized the need for "free agricultural laborers." In 1662, Vice Director William Beekman made it quite clear to Director General Peter Stuyvesant that he would not be able to make the City Colony a success without an adequate supply of African slaves:

> *I solicite most seriously that it may please your honor [Peter Stuyvesant] to accomodate me with a company of negroes, as I am very much in want of them in many respects.*[8]

In 1678, after English leadership ruled the colony, town authorities in New Castle found that even the large influx of English settlers and white indentured servants were not adequate to help the colony survive or prosper. In other words, they too concluded like so many other English settlements "that they could not survive, much less prosper, without the support of Negro slave labor."[9] "In sum, the efforts of the colonies' African population, whether voluntary or not, made major contributions to the growth of the colonies."[10]

What some historians have erroneously described as "runaways" were in fact "truants," slaves or servants who ran away from their masters just to hide away in the vast undiscovered and mostly undisturbed wilderness and/or thickets of forest or swamp areas. They would hide undiscovered for weeks, months, and even years depending upon the severity of the situation they were avoiding. Since many of the African slaves that were brought to this Delaware Colony came from other areas with very different terrains, many just didn't know where to go or what to do after getting there. Others, who were fortunate to have other kin or tribesmen with them, simply weighed "the blessings of freedom against the loss of family and friends."[11] Some of these truants morphed into "maroons," forming self-sustaining communities that eventually grew into villages and towns.[12]

Maroon runaway slave.

There have been reported cases of female slaves going into hiding with the blessings and knowledge of their escape by the master's wife or mistress. Even though many of these cases were self-serving, where the wife or mistress was able to gain much more attention from the master during the female slave's absence, this was still a win-win benefit for both women involved.

Turning my attention to Africans who contributed the most to the establishment of colonial settlements and agricultural life, I found that there were very few who were singled out, such as Black Anthony. Instead, I found labor groups which were identified as contributing greatly to colonial life. The two primary labor groups were seamen and those who could pilot small boats and vessels along the rivers and streams, and house servants and those who represented the master in certain trading transactions. One of the earliest noted African seamen and former indentured servants in the area was Matthias de Souza, who was a mulatto of African and European descent (possibly Portuguese). He worked for Jesuit priests in Maryland along the Chesapeake Bay and eastern shores of Maryland. He came to Maryland in 1634 and was granted his freedom in 1638. He became an accomplished seaman and used his skills to sail the rivers trading with Native Americans, later becoming the master of a ketch belonging to the provincial secretary, John Lewger. He was also known as the first person of color to serve in the colonial Maryland legislature in 1642.[13] As I read his history, I kept seeing the similarities between him and Black Anthony. And just like Anthony, after Matthias' time in the Maryland legislature, there are no records of his whereabouts or of his activities. Here again is an example of

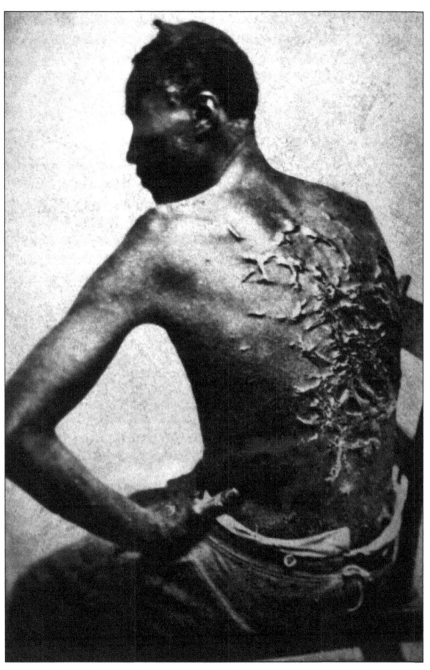
Severe lash marks from whipping.

a free African with position in a colonial European settlement and with ties to Native American tribes who suddenly disappeared from European records of that time.

Africans, free or enslaved, who worked in manufacturing or ship-building were rarely cited for their individual contributions due to the many different hands needed to produce manufactured products or to complete the building of a ship. Another reason for down-playing the importance or special skills of Africans in these two industries was to remove positive role models from the ranks of those free or enslaved Africans desiring more out of life. This is not to say that some free Africans did not excel in those industries, but a researcher would be hard-pressed to find the details of it, except as a posting for a "runaway."

Prior to 1700, many laws and slave codes had been passed and enforced throughout the English colonies to restrict and control the movement of slaves as well as the freedom of non-servitude Africans, with the passage of the dreaded *Fugitive Slave Laws* being among the most oppressive. Prior to the need for fugitive slave laws, Dutch and English settlements were able to unilaterally benefit each other by agreeing to return runaway slaves that were found in their colony.[14] This was mainly possible due to the relatively small percentage of slaves living amongst settlers at that time. As the demand for slaves began to rise disproportionately to their increase in number, the reciprocity spirit of returning runaway slaves began to wane. Adding to that unwillingness to return fugitive slaves was a growing community of slavery opponents who had successfully raised the issue of not having and maintaining slaves at all. Their deep-rooted religious convictions were the basis for changes to the early establishment of legalized slavery among the New England colonies—Massachusetts (1641), Rhode Island (1643)[15]—which Rhode Island outlawed in 1652, yet maintained some of the strictest slave codes in New England.[16]

My reason for mentioning legalized slavery and the slave codes in New England is to help you understand the juxtaposition of the Delaware Colony to the slave societies that existed to the north and to the south, and to further dramatize the conflicting position it presented to this area. The social pressure of not only having "accepted" slavery, but also "necessary" slavery in the South became the mindset for colonists in the two lower counties of the Delaware Colony. In much the same way, "tolerating" slavery yet working towards its "abolishment" became the mindset of the northern-most county, New Castle. Ironically, even though the two areas were in opposition to each other, the need

17ᵗʰ century servant boy.

to limit and restrict the movement of slaves and free Africans was mutually agreeable to all counties. So, even in those early stages of slavery's introduction to the Delaware Colony, the groundwork was being laid for the acceptance and implementation of "Jim Crow" attitudes toward black Africans. Understanding the genesis of racial prejudice and bigotry in those formative years of class servitude should help explain some of the deep-seated attitudes of that social malady, which still exists.

Examining the role of house servants—cooks, chambermaids, maids, nannies, wet nurses, midwives, butlers, trusted coachmen, musicians, blacksmiths[17]—I found that little or no recognition was given to them, even though many of them provided the greatest service and represented the greatest value to their masters. On too many occasions, these slaves and servants (considered closest to the master and his family) helped uncover numerous acts and plots of slave rebellion and insurrection and large numbers of runaways. They looked out for the master and his family, in many cases, more than they looked out for their own family and tribesmen. Although it was several centuries later, Malcolm X was known to have summed up that relationship between master and house servant in a quote that clearly dramatized the love and caring felt by house servants toward their masters. He is quoted as saying that the house Negro [house servant] often cared for the master more than the master cared for himself. When the master would get sick, the house slave was known to say, "What's the matter boss, we sick?"[18]

Another dimension to the house servant/slave-to-master relationship was the undeniable blood connections that existed. In the late half of the 17th century, many female slaves-for-life were "bedded" by their masters as almost a "rite of passage" from virginity to womanhood. The babies born of these sexual encounters were kept close to the master's house, unless it was a very small farmstead with only a few slaves. In that case, regardless of bloodline, nearly everyone had to work the fields and tend the house. Furthermore, regardless of the number of slaves held by a slave owner, his bastard children, more often than not, received favorable treatment.

They wore better clothing, ate better food and lived under better conditions than the other slaves, and received education, training and travel opportunities not afforded to other slaves. In many instances, the boys (much more often than the girls) were emancipated and sent north to study and live as free individuals. Despite all of these preferred treatments, many of these "white-fathered slave children" still were labeled as slaves; nevertheless, several of these slaves were freed as young adults and were able to lead successful lives.[19]

There is no question in fact or history that these umbilical relationships between house slave and master existed from the very origins of chattel slavery. Why? Because indentured servants who served for a limited period (4-7years) did not share the life experiences of growing up with a plantation owner or his family. Being obligated to a family for your entire lifetime develops an enormous commitment that could be either good or bad, but in most cases it was good—for the master. Yet, laudable accounts of these trusted and valued slaves and their obvious contributions to the community in which they lived are all but non-existent during the 17th century, but much more available during the 18th and 19th centuries.[20]

My efforts to find black servants and/or slaves who lived within Southern Pennsylvania and the Three Lower Counties and who became self-made men like Anthony Johnson of Virginia[21] were unproductive. Anthony Johnson's story is well-documented and detailed in a way that is almost uncharacteristic for that period. Yet, at the same time, you would expect to find others just as well-documented and detailed in other colonies, such as the Delaware Colony. Again, the fact that I was not successful in finding more like Johnson in Southern Pennsylvania and the Three Lower Counties during the mid-to-late 1700s does not mean that those free black men like Johnson did not exist. In fact, I believe that Maryland and Virginia's eastern shore plantations and townships were able to preserve the history of notable free Africans better because the area was much more stable than the areas that later became Delaware, which suffered many land-control changes in a very short period of time. These changes in European control between the Dutch, English and Swedes provided many opportunities for written and oral records to be destroyed or lost. The Eastern Shore area, on the other hand, stayed under English rule from its inception; therefore, records of all types were better maintained and preserved. Other examples of self-made Africans were found in Virginia's Northampton County during the mid-17th century, 1640-1676. The records there showed that a number of Africans were able to buy their freedom and establish themselves as small farmers and planters as indicated in the passage below.

> *They became part of a complex human network, and it was their success in dealing with white planters, great and small, servants and slaves, that in large measure explains their viability.... In Northampton County between 1664 and 1677, ten of fifty-three black males were free householders. These free blacks lived like the whites who were not of the wealthiest class. They owned land, grew crops, raised livestock, traded, argued in the courts,*

and had broad social relationships, some legal and moral and some not. But the number of blacks, free or serving, remained small through mid-century.[22]

The introduction of institutionalized racial slavery not only broke the back of a unified working class of poor whites, black Africans, servants and slaves rebelling against the colonial government and large plantation owners, but it also stole from an emerging group of extremely talented and resourceful Africans the God-given equal right to compete for a rightful place in this new world. This was the second most injurious episode in colonial slavery, one which still boldly portrays itself today.

But this book is not about the downside of slavery. It is about those few free Africans who, with the help of the Swedes, Finns, Quakers and Mennonites, were able to rise above the orneriness of hypocritical leaders and designers of this dehumanizing slavery condition in the American colonies. Furthermore, this book is in celebration of the many men and women of the Swedish Nation—which sprung from the New Sweden Colony—and those morally committed Quakers and Mennonites who refused to allow the indecencies of racial slavery to overrule the moral conscientiousness of decent men and women in its path.[23]

It is left for me to mention that free Africans were able to make a substantial contribution to the building of this nation and to the counties later to be known as the State of Delaware as skilled craftsmen—bricklayers, carpenters, cement workers, boot and shoe makers, blacksmiths, and more.

During the William Penn government era of the late 1600s, many Africans who came or were brought to Philadelphia became skilled workers because of the commercial environment that was rapidly developing there. Many of them helped to build several of this area's finest and most historic buildings. One of those notable buildings was Old Swedes Church, which was built next to what was once Fort Christina.

In 1698, it is reported in the church records of Holy Trinity (Old Swedes) Church that the church contracted with Joseph Yard of Philadelphia to complete the masonry work for the church's walls and foundation. One of his workers was a free Negro by the name of Dick, who stayed at the home of John Stalcop, the church warden, while completing his work on the church. It is reported that Negro Dick "knew best how to prepare and carry the mortar."[24] For anyone who is unfamiliar with doing masonry work, the mortar is the most important part of laying the bricks or stones. If the mortar mixture is wrong, the bricks or stones will not hold together. Therefore, it is pretty safe to infer that Negro Dick was a very skilled masonry worker, even though he was paid less than the others. There were several other African laborers who helped build both Old Swedes churches in Wilmington and Philadelphia. Unfortunately, the records do not show whether the other Africans were skilled workers or just laborers at the site.[25]

IN SUMMATION

So far in this book, I've tried to explain the Swedish people's view of slavery and servitude in general, the presence of forced servitude in their midst, the ways in which they managed to deal with it, the undeniable evidence of more than one African in New Sweden and the role played by the Swedes and others to eliminate this inhumane treatment of other human beings. For the most part, the information I have presented is not only my attempt to tell a story others have failed to tell, but also to challenge readers to rethink much of what has been taken for granted about Africans and/or simply not known about them during the early development of colonial America. During the earliest decades of Dutch, English and Swedish history in North America, the records show that the men and women from these three diverse European communities came with very different agendas and goals. The Dutch came with a goal to profit in any way they could. Their purpose for building colonies was an effort to establish nothing more than trading posts and supply areas for the rest of the colonies.[26] Their desire to establish permanent settlements was a last-ditch attempt to hold on to the land they had eked out for their commercial enterprise.

The English came with a similar desire to achieve wealth and riches in order to live a better life, but they were also running away from unfavorable doctrines. Many in the first groups of settlers to arrive had no idea how to be self-sufficient in a wilderness environment, and they failed badly. However, what was hard-wired into their social DNA was the ability to get others to toil for them in whatever capacity they themselves were incapable or unwilling to perform. As a result, England became the first nation to rely heavily on servants in these colonies, transporting a staggering 70-85% of settlers as indentured servants, convict servants and slaves.[27] The goal of the English was to "out-populate" all of the other colonial empires in the New World in order to take control of this land's wealth and natural resources. From their very first attempt at colonizing this land in 1607, the wealth of these lands was discovered and desired:

> *English settlers found a temperate climate and land that was abundant, fertile, and thinly populated. The mildnesse of the aire, the fertilitie of the soile, and the situation of the rivers, wrote John Smith in a Map of Virginia (1612), are so propitious to the nature and use of man as no place is more convenient for pleasure, profit, and man's sustenance.[28]*

What developed from that point forward is all a matter of history, which is etched into the very fabric of the American social consciousness.

Unlike both the Dutch and the English, the Swedes (with several Finns in their settlement groups) came for the sole purpose of establishing a permanent settlement that they planned to develop with a complete set of instructions from their government on what to do and what not to do.[29] They came prepared to settle the wilderness of

North America as self-sufficient and self-reliant farmers with little or no wealth to purchase or barter for servants or slaves.[30] These very resourceful farmers and craftsmen not only survived the harshness of the wilderness and weather, but also the unpredictability of the Native Americans. The Swedish were the only colonists not to have a history of Indian wars or any type of protracted Indian disputes. In sharp contrast to their Dutch and English rivals, the Swedes were admired by the Lenape for their resourcefulness and toughness. In testimony to their respectability and propitiousness as a people were their gracious invitations from both conquering governments of the Dutch and the English to remain in the new colony with their land and possessions intact, and to retain their place in government and in the courts.[31] After transitioning from a colony of their own—New Sweden—to accepting allegiance under the Dutch and English rule and becoming the Swedish Nation, Swedes and Finns in collaboration with Quakers and Mennonites from Hoerenkil (Lewes) to the shores of the Schuylkill River quietly exerted their resistance to slavery and their resistance to all forms of returning runaway slaves.[32] Their combined actions are perhaps the clearest indication I have found to justify their efforts as the definitive predecessors to the abolitionist movement. Many consider the era after 1760 as having given birth to the abolitionist movement; but if you would give careful reading and thought to what I have written on the pre-1700 history of this subject, I believe you will find reason to agree with me that the abolitionist movement actually started much sooner than the commonly accepted date.

As for Africans coming to this European-colonizing territory (more not willing than those willing), they became the unsung and invisible shapers of the Atlantic seaboard colonies. Free or enslaved, they endured the harshest of torture, persecution, denial, and subjugation; yet they were still able to gain equal footing with those who never endured such subjugation. They excelled in skilled areas of crafts, manufacturing and seamanship that were previously unknown in their motherlands. The African Diaspora reached into every corner and aspect of colonial life. The genesis of racial slavery became the precursor for institutionalized racism in this country. The fear held by many government officials and influential landowners of exposing the exceptional talents of many gifted Africans may mean that we will never truly know the far-reaching extent of the African contribution to the establishment of colonial America. What is known are many of the areas in which the African legacy was not hidden or denied, but simply kept to a minimum. And even the minimum that has been revealed so far will someday inspire and motivate others to dig further and/or to release more of what has been hidden for centuries. It is the mission of this book to shed light on the previously unknown contribution of the African presence in the 17th-century Delaware River Valley and the area later to be known as the Delmarva Peninsula. It is also the hope of this author that what I have written will motivate others to use it as a launching pad for greater and further study of this topic.

Endnotes

CHAPTER ONE - SLAVERY IN THE SWEDISH COMMUNITY

1. *Swedish slave trade*, Viking and pre-Viking slavery, http://en.wikipedia.org/wiki/Swedish_slave_trade#Viking_and_pre-Viking_slavery.

2. Scandia was a name used for various uncharted islands in Northern Europe by the first Greek and Roman geographers.

3. *Swedish slave trade*, Viking and pre-Viking slavery, http://en.wikipedia.org/wiki/Swedish_slave_trade#Viking_and_pre-Viking_slavery; & *Thrall*, http://en.wikipedia.org/wiki/Thralls.

4. Ibid.

5. Madeleine Burnside, *Spirits of the Passage*, (1999), 22; European exploration of Africa, http://en.wikipedia.org/wiki/ European_exploration_of_Africa.

6. *Swedish Colonial Empire*, Legacy, http://www.newworldencyclopedia.org/entry/Swedish_colonial_empire#Legacy.

7. *Kalmar Union*, http://en.wikipedia.org/wiki/Kalmar_Union.

8. William H. Williams, *Slavery and Freedom in Delaware, 1639-1865*, 3.

9. *Swedish Gold Coast*, http://en.wikipedia.org/wiki/Swedish_Gold_Coast.

10. Ibid.

11. William H. Williams, *Slavery and Freedom in Delaware, 1639-1865*, 3.

12. Ibid.

13. *Thirty Years' War*, http://en.wikipedia.org/wiki/Thirty_years_war. It was fought in what is now present day Germany from 1618-1648 and involved most of the European countries at that time. The War had raged for so long some had lost sight of its initial cause or its goal; however, most historians believe it began as a religious conflict between Protestants and Catholics in the Holy Roman Empire.

14. The New Sweden Company had been known by many names prior to this one. The first company was established in 1626-27 as the Swedish South Company and later the name was changed in the 18th century to the Swedish West India Company; *Delaware: A Guide to the First State*, (Federal Writers' Project), 21-22.

15. *Swedish Gold Coast*, http://en.wikipedia.org/wiki/Swedish_Gold_Coast.

16. *Swedish slave trade*, http://en.wikipedia.org/wiki/Swedish_slave_trade.

16a. This is reference to the large numbers of white indentured servants and convicts who were sent to the colonies, later freed, given land and status.

17. *1688 Germantown Quaker Petition Against Slavery*, The Issue of Slavery, http://en.wikipedia.org/wiki/The_1688_Germantown_Quaker_Petition_Against_Slavery#The_issue_of_slavery.

Chapter Two - Building New Sweden: Conscience versus Culture

1. Peter Minuit worked for the Dutch, but was not Dutch by birth. He was born in Wesel, Germany as a French Walloon. He is best known for his purchase of the island of Manhattan for the equivalent of $24 (based on a 19th century estimate).

2. John Munroe, *History of Delaware*, 21.

3. Jehu Curtis Clay, *The Annals of the Swedes on the Delaware*, http://archive.org/details/annalsofswedes00clay.

4. Ibid.

5. Matthew T. Mellon, *Early American Views on Negro Slavery*, 8.

6. Ibid., 9.

7. *Swedish slave trade*, Viking and pre-Viking slavery, http://en.wikipedia.org/wiki/Swedish_slave_trade#Viking_and_pre-Viking_slavery.

8. *Swedish Colonial Empire*, Legacy, http://www.newworldencyclopedia.org/entry/Swedish_colonial_empire#Legacy.

9. Saidiya Hartman, *Lose Your Mother*, 19.

10. Charles L. Blockson, *African Americans in Pennsylvania, 13.*

11. G. Soulsman, "The Ugly Truth of Slavery and Church", *The News Journal, Sunday Life F1-2,* (Oct. 24, 2010).

12. Jehu Curtis Clay, *The Annals of the Swedes on the Delaware,* 20-23, http://archive.org/details/annalsofswedes00clay.

13. *Economic Aspects of Tobacco During the Colonial Period 1612–1776,* http://www.tobacco.org/History/colonialtobacco.html.

14. Gary B. Nash, *Red, White & Black: The Peoples of Early North America,* 50.

15. New York Historical Records, 21; & *Collection of Royal Orders and Decrees, Vol. II* (Royal Archives at Stockholm, Sweden).

16. *Economic Aspects of Tobacco During the Colonial Period 1612–1776,* http://www.tobacco.org/History/colonialtobacco.html.

17. C. A. Weslager, *New Sweden on the Delaware: 1638-1655,* 95.

18. Ibid.

Chapter Three - The Role of Africans in New Sweden

1. Thomas J. Scharf, *The History of Delaware, 1609-1888,* 32.

2. Peter S. Craig, *The 1693 Census of the Swedes on the Delaware;* Clas Johansson was one of the soldiers who came aboard the *Kalmar Nyckel* in 1637-38 and remained in

New Sweden. In 1693 his descendants were known as Johnsons in present Pennsylvania and as Classons in present Delaware and Maryland.

3. *Delaware: A Guide to the First State*, (Federal Writers' Project), 23; John A. Munroe, *History of Delaware*, 21; John A. Munroe, *Colonial Delaware*, 17.

4. Peter M. Voelz, *Slave and Soldier*, 37.

5. Ibid.

6. Amandus Johnson, *The Swedish Settlements on the Delaware*, 486.

7. John A. Munroe, *History of Delaware*, 21.

8. Thomas J. Scharf, *History of Delaware, 1609-1888*, 32.

9. William H. Williams, *Slavery & Freedom in Delaware, 1639-1865*, 3.

10. Peter Craig, & Kim-Eric Williams, *Colonial Records of the Swedish Churches in Pennsylvania, Volumes I & II*.

11. Amandus Johnson, *The Swedish Settlements on the Delaware*, 506.

12. John A. Munroe, *Colonial Delaware*, 28; *Delaware: A Guide to the First State*, (Federal Writers' Project), 26.

13. John A. Munroe, *Colonial Delaware*, 31.

14. *New Sweden History*, Vol. II, chapt. LXIII (Royal Archive, Stockholm).

15. John A. Munroe, *History of Delaware*, 17.

16. *Delaware: A Guide to the First State*, (Federal Writers' Project), 23; John A. Munroe, *History of Delaware*, 21; John A. Munroe, *Colonial Delaware*, 17

17. Amandus Johnson, *The Swedes in America, 1638–1900*, 87.

18. Ibid., 89.

19. William Dillon Piersen, *From Africa to America*, 68.

CHAPTER FOUR - WHAT BECAME OF ANTONI SWART AND OTHERS LIKE HIM?

1.*Economic Aspects of Tobacco During the Colonial Period 1612–1776*, http://www.tobacco.org/History/colonialtobacco.html.

2. Douglas Weeks, *Blacks in Time*, 16, 22; *Slavery in Colonial America*, http://www.absoluteastronomy.com/topics/Slavery_in_Colonial_America. These Africans were brought to Jamestown, Virginia aboard a Dutch slave ship coming from the West Indies.

3. Oscar Reiss, *Blacks in Colonial America*, 90.

4. *Delaware: A Guide to the First State*, (Federal Writers' Project), 45.

5. Oscar Reiss, *Blacks in Colonial America*, 79.

6. A way of referring to commercial mercenaries and a nicer way of referring to a pirate.

7. William Dillon Piersen, *From Africa to America*, 62.

8. Albany Records, quoted in the Breviat in Case of Penn and Lord Baltimore, 35; S. Hazard, *Annals of Pennsylvania*, 49.

9. William H. Williams, *Slavery and Freedom in Delaware*, 6.

10. Oscar Reiss, *Blacks in Colonial America*, 79.

11. The Riksdaler, the Florijn and the copper money were always reduced to Dalers silver money in the official journal of the company, and the salaries of the officers in the employ of the company in Sweden were paid in "Daler s.m."; *Currency, Coin use in the 17th Century.* http://www.rootsweb.ancestry.com/~nycoloni/nswcoin.html; Amandus Johnson, *Swedish Settlements on the Delaware*, (1911), 41.

12. Since Anthony was the special assistant to Governor Printz, he would have traveled with him all over the colony and he would have been very familiar to everyone there.

13. John H. Franklin, *From Slavery To Freedom 9th Edition*, 65.

14. *Changes in Servitude*, http://score.rims.k12.ca.us/score_lessons/slavery/pages/changes_servitude.html

15. William H. Williams, *Slavery and Freedom in Delaware*, 162.

16. Ibid, 6-7. Dutch slave ships supplied not only the colonies of the Dutch West India Company with seasoned as well as green Africans, but also the Eastern Shore colonies of Maryland and Virginia.

17. *1654 Eagle - New Sweden Immigrants*, http://www.rootsweb.ancestry.com/~nycoloni/shsw9orn.html; John A. Munroe, *Colonial Delaware*, 30; C. A. Weslager, *The Swedes and Dutch At New Castle*, 90.

18. Oscar Reiss, *Blacks in Colonial America*, 80.

19. Ibid., 79.

20. "Germantown Petition," (1688). Original at the Haverford College Library in Quaker & Special Colections. The Petition was first submitted to the Abington Monthly Meeting, then to the Philadelphia Quarterly Meeting and finally to the Yearly Meeting, where it was rejected. *1688 Germantown Quaker Petition Against Slavery*, The issure of slavery, http://en.wikipedia.org/wiki/The_1688_Germantown_Quaker_Petition_Against_Slavery#The_issue_of_slavery.

21. Dorothy & Carl J. Schneider, *Slavery in America*, 247.

22. Ibid., 190.

23. William H. Williams, *Slavery and Freedom in Delaware*, 146.

24. *1688 Germantown Quaker Petition Against Slavery*, The issue of slavery, http://en.wikipedia.org/wiki/The_1688_Germantown_Quaker_Petition_Against_Slavery#The_issue_of_slavery.

25. Thomas J. Scharf, *History of Delaware*, Chapter IV, 30.

26. In 1785, King Gustav III established a Swedish colony on the island of Saint-Barthélemy and made it a center for facilitating slave trades. In addition, many Swedish medalists and blacksmiths established lucrative businesses making the irons, chains and other restraints used by purveyors and owners of slaves.

27. William H. Williams, *Slavery and Freedom in Delaware*, 146

Chapter Five - The Dutch Influence on Africans in New Sweden

1. C. A. Weslager,*The Swedes and Dutch At New Castle*, 157.

2. John A. Munroe, *Colonial Delaware*, 41.

3. William H. Williams, *Slavery and Freedom in Delaware*, 6.

4. Edwin G. York, *Opportunity Valley*, 125.

5. Ibid., 43.

6. Ira Berlin, *Slavery in New York,* 41-42.

7. Peter M. Voelz, *Slave and Soldier*,104.

8. Opportunity Valley, York, Edwin, p. 42, History of Delaware, Munroe, J. pps. 15-16.

9. Oscar Reiss, *Blacks in Colonial America*, 97.

10. Ibid., 80; Franklin & Higginbotham, *From Slavery to Freedom: A History of African Americans*, 27.

11. "slavery buffer zone" - my way of describing an area between slave-holding areas where slavery was not practiced.

12. William Dillon Piersen, *From Africa to America*, 68.

13. Oscar Reiss, *Blacks in Colonial America*, 8.

13a. William H. Williams, *Slavery and Freedom in Delaware*, 10.

14. Ibid.; Donald R. Wright, *African Americans in the Colonial Era: From African Origins Through the American Revolution*, 47 & 53.

15. Constance J. Cooper, *350 Years of New Castle, Delaware*, 23; C. A. Weslager, *Dutch Explorers, Traders and Settlers in the Delaware Valley*, 244.

16. Oscar Reiss, *Blacks in Colonial America*,11.

17. Ibid. It has been reported and confirmed that Ibos and Senegalese Africans had discovered and put into practical application the first known immunization treatment, which accounts for their unusual ability to fend off deadly European sicknesses and diseases.

18. Ibid., 12.

18a. Madeleine Burnside, *Spirits of the Passage*, (1999), 39-40

19. Oscar Reiss, *Blacks in Colonial America*, 12.

19a. Christina Synder, *Slavery in Indian Country: The Changing Face of Captivity in Early America*, 50.

20. John A. Munroe, *Colonial Delaware*,15.

21. *Slavery among Native Americans in the United States*, http://en.wikipedia.org/wiki/Slavery_among_Native_Americans_in_the_United_States

22. *Delaware: A Guide to the First State*, (Federal Writers' Project), 45.

23. William H. Williams, *Slavery and Freedom in Delaware*, 11.

24. William H. Williams, *Slavery and Freedom in Delaware*, 12.

25. Oscar Reiss, *Blacks in Colonial America*, 90; Donald R. Wright, *African Americans in the Colonial Era: From African Origins Through the American Revolution*, 73; *Slavery in Pennsylvania*, Slavery in the North, http://www.slavenorth.com/pennsylvania.htm.

26. Oscar Reiss, *Blacks in Colonial America*, 90-91.

27. *Slavery in Pennsylvania*, Slavery in the North, http://www.slavenorth.com/pennsylvania.htm; Oscar Reiss, *Blacks in Colonial America*, 90.

28. William H. Williams, *Slavery and Freedom in Delaware*, xii; E. Becker, *Chronology of the History of Slavery: 1619-1789*, http://innercity.org/holt/slavechron.html.

CHAPTER SIX - THE ENGLISH INFLUENCE ON SWEDISH SETTLERS

1. John H. Franklin, *From Slavery to Freedom 3ʳᵈ Edition*, 90; *Newsletter of Capt. W. H.McCauley*, http://www.scvcamp260.org/newsletter/2007/2007-03-JulyAug-NL.pdf, 8.

2. John H. Franklin, *From Slavery To Freedom 9ᵗʰ Edition,* 51.

3. Oscar Reiss, *Blacks in Colonial America*, 98.

4. *Slavery in Colonial America*, http://www.absoluteastronomy.com/topics/Slavery_in_Colonial_America; John H. Franklin, *From Slavery To Freedom 9ᵗʰ Edition*, 51.

5. John H. Franklin, *From Slavery To Freedom 9ᵗʰ Edition*, 55-56; *Chapter 04 - American Life in the 17ᵗʰ Century*, http://www.course-notes.org/us_history/notes/the_american_pageant_10th_edition_textbook_notes/chapter_4_american_life_in_the_17t; Oscar Reiss, *Blacks in Colonial America*, 99.

6. *Africans in the 17ᵗʰ Century*, http://socyberty.com/history/africans-in-the-17th-century/#ixzz1n3FStinW.

7. Oscar Reiss, *Blacks in Colonial America*, 105.

8. George Washington Williams (October 16, 1849 – August 2, 1891) was an American Civil War veteran, minister, politician and historian. He was the author of the first history book on the history of African-Americans in this country, *The History of the Negro Race in America 1619–1880*.

9. John H. Franklin, *From Slavery To Freedom 9ᵗʰ Edition*, 55.

10. Donald R. Wright, *African Americans in the Colonial Era: From African Origins Through the American Revolution*, 76.

11. Ibid.

12. William H. Williams, *Slavery and Freedom in Delaware*, 1.

13. William H. Williams, *Slavery and Freedom in Delaware*, 12.

14. A land tax imposed by Parliament of two shillings per one hundred acres of land.

15. William H. Williams, *Slavery and Freedom in Delaware*, 11; Dale Taylor, *Everyday Life in Colonial America*, 33.

Chapter Seven - African Contributions In and Around the Swedish Settlement: 1639-1700

1. Timothy J. Shannon, *Atlantic Lives*, 127.

2. *Africans in the 17th Century*, http://socyberty.com/history/africans-in-the-17th-century/#ixzz1n3FStinW.

3. Oscar Reiss, *Blacks in Colonial America*, 192.

4. Ibid., 194-195.

5. Refer to Chapter VI – *The English Influence on Swedish Settlers*.

6. C. A. Weslager, *The Swedes and Dutch at New Castle*, 42.

7. William D Piersen, *From Africa to America*, 56.

8. William H. Williams, *Slavery and Freedom in Delaware*, 1.

9. William D Piersen, *From Africa to America*, 64.

10. Dale Taylor, *Everyday Life in Colonial America*, 235.

11. William H. Williams, *Slavery and Freedom in Delaware*,163.

12. Oscar Reiss, *Blacks in Colonial America*, 190-191.

13. *The Black Past: Remembered and Reclaimed*, de Souza, Matthias, http://www.blackpast.org/?q=aah/de-souza-matthias-circa-1642 (2/21/2012)

14. Oscar Reiss, *Blacks in Colonial America*, 193.

15. Oscar Reiss, *Blacks in Colonial America*, 66; William H. Williams, *From Slavery to Freedom 3rd Edition*, 101-102.

16. William H. Williams, *Slavery and Freedom in Delaware*, 74.

17. William H. Williams, *Slavery and Freedom in Delaware*, 142; Dorothy & Carl J. Schneider, *Slavery in America*, 113-114. Many of the specialized jobs listed above were not in a typical Delaware Colony plantation, but did exist in a few. Many of these positions were more common during the 18th century.

18. *Malcom X*, http://malcolmxfiles.blogspot.com.

19. *Slavery in America: The Masters' Children and Other Mulattos*, http://histclo.com/act/work/slave/am/machi/machi.html; John H. Franklin, *From Slavery to Freeedom 3rd Edition*, 205.

20. *Slavery in America: The Masters' Children and Other Mulattos*, http://histclo.com/act/work/slave/am/machi/machi.html.

21. Donald R. Wright, *African Americans in the Colonial Era: From African Origins Through the American Revolution*, 51; Oscar Reiss, *Blacks in Colonial America*, 99 & 132; *From Indentured Servitude to Racial Slavery*, http://www.pbs.org/wgbh/aia/part1/1narr3.html.

22. Donald R. Wright, *African Americans in the Colonial Era: From African Origins Through the American Revolution*, 51; T. H. Breen, *Myne Owne Ground: Race and Freedom on Virginia's Eastern Shore, 1640-1676*, 68.

23. John H. Franklin, *From Slavery To Freedom 9th Edition*, 96 & 99; Oscar Reiss, *Blacks in Colonial America*, 95; William H. Williams, *Slavery and Freedom in Delaware*, 6.

24. The Records of Holy Trinity (Old Swedes) Church, 30.

25. Dr. Kim-Eric Williams, *Africans and the Swedes*.

26. William H. Williams, *Slavery and Freedom in Delaware*, 6.

27. John H. Franklin, *From Slavery To Freedom 9th Edition*, 146.

28. Donald R. Wright, *African Americans in the Colonial Era: From African Origins Through the American Revolution*, 49-50.

29. Jehu Curtis Clay, *The Annals of the Swedes on the Delaware*, 20-23, http://archive.org/details/annalsofswedes00clay.

30. Dr. Kim-Eric Williams, *Africans and the Swedes*; C. A. Weslager, *New Sweden on the Delaware*, Weslager, 81-83; Amandus Johnson, *The Swedish Settlements on the Delaware*, 499-500.

31. John A. Munroe, *History of Delaware*, 27 & 30;

32. Ibid., 35; *Delaware: A Guide to the First State*, (Federal Writers' Project), 33.

Bibliography

Åberg, Alf & Kultur, Natur Och. *The People of New Sweden: Our Colony on the Delaware River*, The Royal Library: Stockholm, Sweden, 1988.

Battle, Thomas C. & Wells, Donna M. editors. *LEGACY: Treasures of Black History*, National Geographic Society: Washington, D.C., 2006.

Becker, Eddie. *Chronology of the History of Slavery: 1619-1789*, Holt House Web Site, 1999.

Berlin, Ira & Harris, Leslie M. *Slavery in New York*, The New York Press: New York, NY, 2005.

Blockson, Charles L. *African Americans in Pennsylvania: Above Ground and Underground*, An Illustrated Guide: Harrisburg, PA. 2001.

Blumrosen, Alfred W. & Blumrosen, Ruth G. *Slave Nation: How Slavery United the Colonies & Sparked the American Revolution*, Sourcebooks, Inc.: Naperville, IL, 2005.

Breen, T.H. & Innes, Stephen. *Myne Owne Ground: Race and Freedom on Virginia's Eastern Shore, 1640-1676*, Oxford University Press, Inc.: New York, NY & Oxford, England, 1980.

Burnside, Madeleine. *Spirits of the Passage: The Transatlantic Slave Trade in the Seventeenth Century*, Simon & Schuster Editions: New York, NY, 1997.

Burr, Horace. *The Records of Holy Trinity (Old Swedes) Church, From 1697 to 1773*, Historical Society of Delaware: Wilmington, DE, 1890.

Christensen, Gardell D. & Burney, Eugenia. *Colonial Delaware*, Thomas Nelson Inc.: Nashville, TN, 1974.

Clay, Jehu Curtis. *Annals of the Swedes on the Delaware*, J. C. Penchin: Philadelphia, PA, 1835. (Online)

Cooper, Constance J. *350 Years of New Castle, Delaware: Chapters in a Town's History*, New Castle Historical Society, New Castle, DE & Cedar Tree Books: Wilmington, DE, 2001.

Craig, Peter Stebbins & Williams, Kim-Eric, editors. *Colonial Records of the Swedish Churches in Pennsylvania, Volumes I & II*, Swedish Colonial Society: Philadelphia, PA, 2006.

Davis, Kenneth C. *America's Hidden History*, Harper Collins Publishers: New York, NY, 2008

Delaware Federal Writers' Project (WPA). *New Castle on the Delaware*, New Castle Historical Society: New Castle, DE, 1936.

Dodson, Howard. *The Emergence of African–American Culture: JUBILEE*, The Schomburg Center for Research in Black Culture & National Geographic: Washington, D.C., 2002.

Eskridge, Ann E. *Slave Uprisings and Runaways: Fighting for Freedom and the Underground Railroad*, Enslow Publishers, Inc.: Berkeley Heights, NJ, 2004.

Federal Writers' Project of the Works Progress Administration for Delaware. *Delaware: A Guide to the First State*, The Viking Press: New York, NY, 1938.

Ferris, Benjamin. *A History of the Original Settlements on the Delaware & A History of Wilmington*. Gateway Press, Inc.: Baltimore, MD, 1987 (Reprint of the 1846 Original).

Franklin, John Hope & Higginbotham, Evelyn Brooks. *From Slavery to Freedom: A History of African Americans*, Alfred A. Knopf: New York, NY, Third Edition, 1967.

Franklin, John Hope & Higginbotham, Evelyn Brooks. *From Slavery to Freedom: A History of African Americans*, McGraw-Hill: New York, NY, Ninth Edition, 2011.

Gerbner, Katharine (Harvard University). "Antislavery in Print: the Germantown Protest, the 'Exhortation' and the Seventeenth-Century Quaker Debate on Slavery". Presented at the Quakers and Slavery, 1657-1865 conference, Philadelphia, PA; November 4, 2010

Hartman, Saidiya. *Lose Your Mother: A Journey Along the Atlantic Slave Route*. Farrar, Straus & Giroux: New York, NY, 2007.

Hashaw, Tim. *The Birth of Black America: The First African Americans and the Pursuit of Freedom at Jamestown*, Carroll & Graf Publishers: New York, NY, 2007.

Hoffecker, Carol, E., et al. *New Sweden in America*, Associated University Presses, Inc.: Newark, DE, 1995.

Johnson, Amandus. *The Swedes on the Delaware 1638–1664*, International Printing Company: Philadelphia, PA, 1927.

Johnson, Amandus. *The Swedish Settlements on the Delaware, 1638–1664*, University of Pennsylvania: Philadelphia, PA, 1911.

Johnson, Charles; Smith, Patricia & WGBH Series Research Team. A*fricans in America: America's Journey through Slavery*, HHarcourt Brace & Company: New York, NY, 1998

Kolchin, Peter. *American Slavery, 1619-1877*, Hill and Wang: New York, New York, 1993.

Marks, Carole C., Editor. *A History of African Americans of Delaware and Maryland's Eastern Shore*, Delaware Heritage Press: Wilmington, DE, 1998.

Mellon, Matthew T. *Early American Views on Negro Slavery*, Bergman Publishers: New York, NY, 1934 (1st Edition), 1969 (New Edition).

Morris, Richard B. & Woodress, James. *Voices From America's Past: The Colonies and The New Nation – Volume One*, E.P. Dutton & Co., Inc.: New York, NY, 1963.

Munroe, John A. *Colonial Delaware: A History*, KTO Press: Millwood, New York, 1978.

Munroe, John A. *History of Delaware*, University of Delaware Press: Newark, DE, 1979, 1984.

Nash, Gary B. *Red, White & Black: The Peoples of Early North America*, Prentice Hall: Englewood Cliffs, NJ, 1992, 1982, 1974.

Odhner, Clas Teodor. *The Founding of New Sweden 1637-1642*, The Historical Society of Pennsylvania: Philadelphia, PA, 1879.

Olson, Kay M. *Africans in America, 1619–1865*, Blue Earth Books: Mankato, Minn., 2003.

Piersen, William Dillon. *Black Legacy: America's Hidden Heritage,* The University of Massachusetts Press: Amherst, MA, 1993.

Piersen, William Dillon. *From Africa to America: African American history from the Colonial era to the early Republic, 1526-1790*, Twayne Publishers: Gale Group, New York, NY, 1996.

Purvis, Thomas L. *Colonial America to 1763*, Facts on File, Inc.: New York, NY, 1999.

Reiss, Oscar. *Blacks in Colonial America*, McFarland & Company, Inc.: Jefferson, NC, 1997.

Scharf, J. Thomas. *History of Delaware, 1609-1888,* Philadelphia, PA: L.J. Richards & Company, 1888. Reprinted, Westminster, MD: Family Lines Publications, 1990.

Seybert, Tony. *Slavery and Native Americans in British North America and the United States: 1600 to 1865,* Slavery in America Essay Series; http://www.slaveryinameri-ca.org/history/hs_es_ indians_slavery.htm

Shannon, Timothy J. *Atlantic Lives: A Comparative Approach to Early America,* Pearson Education, Inc.: New York, NY, 2004.

Schneider, Dorothy & Schneider, Carl J. *Slavery in America: From Colonial Times to the Civil War,* Checkmark Books: New York, NY, 2000.

Soulsman, Gary. *The Ugly Truth of Slavery and Church,* Sunday Life F1-2, October 24, 2010, *The News Journal.*

Sonneborn, Liz. *A Primary Source History of the Colony of Maryland,* The Rosen Publishing Group, Inc.: New York, NY, 2006.

Synder, Christina. *Slavery in Indian Country: The Changing Face of Captivity in Early America,* Harvard University Press: Cambridge, MA, 2010.

Taylor, Dale. *Everyday Life in Colonial America,* Writer's Digest Books: Cincinnati, Ohio, 1997.

Thompson, Alvin O. *Flight to Freedom: African Runaways and Maroons in the Americas,* University of the West Indies Press: Kingston, Jamaica, 2006.

Voelz, Peter M. *Slave and Soldier: The Military Impact of Blacks in the Colonial Americas,* Garland Publishing, Inc.: New York & London, 1993.

Weslager, C. A. *Delaware's Forgotten Folk, The Story of the Moors & Nanticokes,* The University of Pennsylvania Press: Philadelphia, PA, 1943.

Weslager, C.A. in collaboration with Dunlap, A. R. *Dutch Explorers, Traders and Settlers in the Delaware Valley, 1609 – 1664,* University of Pennsylvania Press: Philadelphia, PA, 1961.

Weslager, C. A. *New Sweden on the Delaware, 1638-1655,* The Middle Atlantic Press: Wilmington, Delaware, 1988.

Weslager, C. A. *The Swedes and Dutch at New Castle,* The Middle Atlantic Press: Wilmington, Delaware, 1988.

Williams, George Washington. *The History of the Negro Race in America, 1619-1880, Volume I*, G. P. Putnam's Sons: New York, NY, 1883.

Williams, Kim-Eric. *Africans and the Swedes*, an article written for the Swedish Colonial Society Newsletter and website.

Williams, William H. *Slavery and Freedom in Delaware, 1639–1865*. Scholarly Resources Inc.: Wilmington, DE, 1996.

Williams, William H. *The First State: An Illustrated History of Delaware*. Windsor Publications, Inc.: Northridge, CA, 1985.

Wright, Donald R. *African Americans in the Colonial Era: From African Origins Through the American Revolution*. Harlan Davidson, Inc.: Arlington Heights, Illinois, 1990

York, Edwin G. *Opportunity Valley: A History of the Delaware River Valley before 1800*. Edwin G. York, 2007.

INTERNET SOURCES

http://www.absoluteastronomy.com/topics/Slavery_in_Colonial_America (10/10/11)

http://www.afrolumens.org/slavery/buying.html (2/23/12)

http://www.answers.com/topic/triangular-trade (2/23/12)

http://www.archive.org/stream/cu31924092229222/cu31924092229222_djvu.txt

http://www.blackpast.org/?q=aah/de-souza-matthias-circa-1642 (3/5/12)

http://www.britannica.com/EBchecked/topic/576478/Sweden/29856/The-Kalmar-Union?anchor=ref403726

http://www.colonialswedes.org/History/Chronology.html (10/10/11)

http://www.course-notes.org/us_history/notes/the_american_pageant_10th_edition_textbook_ notes/ chapter_4_american_life_in_the_17t (2/13/12)

http://www.slaveryinamerica.org/geography/slave_laws_PA.htm (2/23/12)

http://besthistorysites.net/index.php/american-history/colonial (3/5/12)

http://en.wikipedia.org/wiki/Black_Indians (10/11/11)

http://en.wikipedia.org/wiki/European_exploration_of_Africa (2/12/12) http://en.wikipedia.org/wiki/Kalmar_Union (1/21/13)

http://en.wikipedia.org/wiki/Slavery_among_Native_Americans_in_the_United_States (10/11/11)

http://en.wikipedia.org/wiki/Swedish_Gold_Coast (2/12/12)

http://en.wikipedia.org/wiki/Swedish_slave_trade#Viking_and_pre-Viking_slavery (9/29/11)

http://en.wikipedia.org/w/index.php?title=Swedish_colonial_empire&oldid=217005637

http://en.wikipedia.org/wiki/The_1688_Germantown_Quaker_Petition_Against_ Slavery#The_issue_of_slavery (10/11/11)

http://histclo.com/act/work/slave/am/machi/machi.html (1/26/13)

http://nabbhistory.salisbury.edu/dho/themes/people/index.html (3/2/12)

http://nativeamericansofdelawarestate.com/HeiteReport1.htm (10/11/11)

http://socyberty.com/history/africans-in-the-17th-century/ (2/21/12)

http://www.newrivernotes.com/de/swede.htm (9/29/11)

http://www.newworldencyclopedia.org/entry/Swedish_colonial_empire (2/12/12)

http://www.newworldencyclopedia.org/entry/Swedish_colonial_empire#Legacy (2/12/12)

http://www.npr. org/templates/ story/story. php?storyId= 130489804

http://www.nps.gov/history/ethnography/aah/AAheritage/ChesapeakeA.htm (2/14/12)

http://www.rootsweb.ancestry.com/~nycoloni/nswcoin.html (9/29/11)

http://www.rootsweb.ancestry.com/~nycoloni/shsw9orn.html (9/28/11)

http://www.slavenorth.com/delaware.htm (9/28/11)

http://www.slavenorth.com/pennsylvania.htm (9/28/11)

http://westjersey.org/sjh/sjh_chap_1.htm (9/28/11)

Index

Dutch
  City Colony 57, 58, 60, 61,
    62, 73, 81, 87
  Company Colony 57, 58,
    60, 62
  Dutch privateers 61
  Dutch Reformed Church
    22, 49
  Dutch slave traders 43, 61
  Dutch West India Company
    41, 42, 50, 51, 54, 55, 57,
    58, 60, 81
  Mennonites 21, 22, 50, 51,
    53, 60, 94, 97

E

East Atlantic Islands 31
English
  indentured servants 79, 81,
    96
  landowners 73, 74, 76, 78, 80
  Puritans xi, 21
  slave owners 47
Europeans
  indentured servants ix, 20,
    46, 63, 67, 73, 74, 76, 84,
    85, 87
  runaway 45

F

Falls of Sanhickan (or Sanki-
  kan) 17
Ferken's Creek 17
Finns 13, 17, 18, 19, 30, 53,
  56, 60, 80, 94, 96, 97
  indentured servants 17
  fugitive slave laws 90

fur trading 83

G

Germantown 53

H

Hudson River Valley 60

I

immunization 103
indentured servants ix, xii, 17,
  19, 20, 35, 42, 44, 46, 48,
  63, 67, 73, 74, 76, 79, 81,
  84, 85, 87, 88, 92, 96.
    See also Africans;
    See also English;
    See also Europeans;
    See also Finns;
    See also Swedish
institutionalized racism 75, 97
intermarriage 70
Iroquois *See Native Americans*

J

Jim Crow 91

K

Kalmar Nyckel 32, 37
King Magnus IV 4
King of Futu 7, 9
Kling, Mans 30

L

land grants 45, 81
Lenape *See Native Americans*
Lewger, John 88
London Company xi

114

About the Author

The author, Abdullah R. Muhammad, is an educator and historian formerly from Baltimore, MD, and Queens, NY, currently residing in Wilmington, Delaware. He is a member of the New Sweden Centre board. He serves as a volunteer re-enactor for our organization in the role of Black Anthony, the first free African in New Sweden Colony in 1639. In addition, he also lectures around the state on this little-known subject.

Upon relocating to Delaware, he learned that his high school students had little interest or knowledge about Delaware's history. This inspired him to create and publish a 2007-2012 Delaware history calendar, including a perpetual calendar providing ready access to important historical events throughout the history of Delaware. This calendar became the #1-selling calendar after 60 days. In conjunction with this unique educational tool, he published *The Making of Delaware One Day at a Time*, an easy-to-read book on the historical events and people in Delaware from 1608 to 2007. This book, with its fresh look at the subject, became the #1-selling history book in the state in 90 days. Also, Abdullah has been honored for his first book by the Wilmington City Council, the New Castle County Council and the State House of Representatives.

Just as he has approached well-known topics with a fresh look, so has he approached this mostly unknown topic of Africans in

New Sweden and the Delaware River Valley. It was in his role as Black Anthony that he was inspired to research the history of Africans in our developing Swedish colony and the rest of the Delaware River Valley, because he found it very hard to believe that Anthony was the only African living in the area. In addition, the mystery that surrounded Anthony's arrival, life and departure from this colony formed the motivation and rationale for writing this book.

The New Sweden Centre website has a brief 10-page PowerPoint presentation of this topic as well as a synopsis of this book accessible to the public at www.colonialnewsweden.org. We invite you to visit it.

Aleasa Hogate
New Sweden Centre VP/Education Director

Colophon

Africans in New Sweden: the Untold Story was designed in Italy by Bob Schwartz on an Apple MacPro using Adobe InDesign and Adobe Photoshop.The text was set in eleven point Berling thirteen point leaded. Chapter titles and running heads were set in Afrika T Ubuntu, Berling and Helvetica Neue.

Berling is a 1951 masterpiece from Swedish designer Karl-Erik Forsberg and Africa T Ubuntu was created in 1999 by Fonts of Africa.

This first edition was digitally printed and bound in the United States of America by Total Printing Systems of Newton, Illinois, on 70# white opaque.